The Alaskan Retreater's Notebook

Cookie

The Alaskan Retreater's Notebook

One Man's Journey
into the Alaskan Wilderness

Ray Ordorica

SKYHORSE PUBLISHING

This book is dedicated to the memory of my dear friend Cookie.

Library of Congress Cataloging-in-Publication Data is available on file.

Cover design by Qualcom
Cover photograph: Thinkstock

ISBN: 978-1-63450-247-4
Ebook ISBN: 978-1-51070-082-6
Printed in China

Contents

Acknowledgments

My first and most profound thanks go to Lennie Fitzpatrick, who had to leave early. Without his kind help I doubt this story would have been written. He gave me the best possible help and a good start on my Alaskan adventures, and I miss him.

Great thanks to Jack and Jan Hansen who went far out of their way to ease my burdens in the bush. Thanks also to Sue and Lance Fitzpatrick, and to the late Andy and Ruthie Runyan, the late Harry Billum, and the late Bob Plouffe. Thanks to Don and Eva MacArthur, Dean and Janet Williams, Fred Lauffenberger, and to Becky and R. B. (Willie) Willie, and even to Paul Kuske. Thanks to Sherman and Peggy Reynolds for their friendship at Red Cabin. All these folks, some of whom have crossed over, helped out this pilgrim and taught him lots about Alaska.

I extend my gratitude to the National Rifle Association for permission to reprint my story, "Guns for the Last Pioneers."

Special thanks to Dr. Jasper I. Lillie and Danny Daniels for moral support all along the way, to Don Fisher who made sure I got my sixguns, and to John Linebaugh who made sure I got 'em back when I left Alaska. Finally, thanks to my old friend Curt Lund who kicked me out into the cold when it was time for me to head north.

Introduction

In the fall of 1978 I packed everything I thought would be useful into my Toyota Land Cruiser and drove north to Alaska. I came to a land I had never seen to find something I wasn't even sure existed: a wilderness cabin to use for a year or more to live, think, relax, read, and write. I found my cabin, fixed it up, and, although it was just an uninsulated twelve-by-sixteen-foot one-room log structure, it was good enough to keep me almost comfortable for three winters.

My life in that cabin fulfilled a dream of more than ten years' standing. I had many problems and made many mistakes, but learned a lot about Alaska. Some of the tools, equipment, and supplies I brought with me were good, some useless. Left behind were some tools and other items that I wished for, many times. I brought whimsical items that turned out to be worth their weight in gold.

It occurred to me that there must be many others who have put off an extended wilderness visit to Alaska out of ignorance or fear. They have as many questions about Alaska as I had before I arrived: How do you cope with 40 below? How do you get water? Is it totally dark in midwinter? And I had a thousand other questions about survival in an icebox.

I'm sure there are many people who would like to "get away" for a spell, for whatever reasons they feel the need to do so. It might be it a simple desire to get away from too much noise, or a need to escape pressures of job or family, or even the desire to build a survival retreat for avoiding any social upheaval that would follow a nuclear confrontation, or what-have-you. These folks might choose interior Alaska for their retreat if they knew how to deal with the unknown terrors of our annual deep-freeze.

If you wish to build a retreat cabin in Alaska, study the maps and all the literature you can get on Alaska, and try to pick where in this extremely vast state you want to live. Pick your locale before you leave your present home. Then come up and have a look around. Fly over the areas you want to see. Many areas of wild Alaska are inaccessible except by aircraft. There's no better way to get the lay of the land than to see it from the air. If possible, camp out in your chosen area. Camp there for as long a time as you can, in as many seasons as possible. I believe the best way to get a feeling for the land is to spend time camping on it. That's probably the fastest way to find out how suitable your area is for year-round habitation.

When you have decided where you want to build, buy the land from whoever owns it. Much of Alaska's land is presently closed to entry due to federal or state restrictions. However, there are good maps available which show you where you can and can't go. Much of the state is privately owned and can be purchased. Some of it can be obtained through state auction, and the authorities in Juneau or Anchorage can give you all the information you need on how to obtain these parcels of land. At the time I lived at Army Point there were even some homesteading plots available, though most of the parcels were mighty remote. Be sure to get a place near good water, and with timber for burning and building.

The problem with a really remote piece of land is how to get your tools, building materials, etc., as well as yourself to the spot to begin building. You can fly in to the nearest lake, which may be miles from your remote parcel. Then you have to figure out how to transport yourself and your equipment to your own parcel of land before you can even start building. However, when you successfully solve all these problems and get your cabin all built, you'll be rewarded with complete solitude . . . if that is what you really want. It is possible to get too remote within Alaska, in that you'll be a very long way from supply centers with no way but air travel to get there.

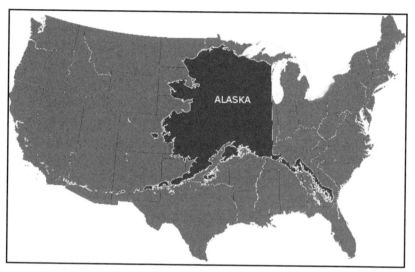

This overlay map shows just how big Alaska really is. From Ketchikan to the tip of the Aleutians spans the distance from Florida to California, and it's as tall as from Texas to North Dakota. Most of Alaska has no roads whatsoever.

I don't claim to be an expert on Alaskan survival conditions. However, I know a helluva lot more now than I did some years ago when I was sitting on my duff in Denver, having never seen Alaska. There is only so much one can learn from books, first-hand experience being the better teacher. Much of what I have to say in this book is based on the premise of solitary living. I moved to Alaska alone, with no family. You may settle in an area where there are many close neighbors to help you out. I got lots of help from my few neighbors, though I didn't plan on it. I think that any preparations you make to come and live in the north should be based on being as self-sufficient as possible, within your group.

Self-sufficiency precludes borrowing, though some of this is inevitable. This means you'll have to bring many things with you, or plan to buy them in one of the supply centers like Anchorage or Fairbanks when you arrive.

What to bring? It's impossible to answer this question to everyone's complete satisfaction. Obviously you'll need more tools—and different kinds of tools — if you plan to build your own cabin, or homestead and "prove up," than you'll need if you want to buy someone's existing cabin. Some of the problems are universal. I hope to provide some useful insight and hints in this book to help those who are more or less seriously considering retreating to Alaska.

Learn to live with the country, not against it, and you'll come to love Alaska.

Cold and Clothes

Undoubtedly the biggest deterrent to coming north forever is the cold. No matter where you now live (outside of Alaska), go into your local supermarket, stop Mabel Housewife in the soup aisle, and ask her what she thinks of Alaska. Chances are she'll tell you, "It's cold up there!" It makes no difference that the farthest north she has been is Peoria, she knows just how miserable it is in Alaska.

"Doesn't everyone know it's cold in Alaska? They all live in igloos up there!" Ignorance about Alaska abounds throughout the lower forty-eight states.

One winter before I came to Alaska, when I still lived in Denver, I used to sit and watch the Anchorage temperatures posted on the evening news. For weeks on end it was consistently warmer in Anchorage than in Denver. Denver winters were a piece of cake compared to the Ohio and Michigan winters I had shivered through during my school days, so I knew before I got to Alaska that at least the Anchorage weather held no unknown terrors for me.

Anyone can cope with a lot of the weather one finds along the coast in the southern part of Alaska. The weather is relatively mild in this area south of the Chugach range from Anchorage down the southeast coastline towards Juneau. Those areas, as well as Kodiak and the surrounding islands, the Kenai and Alaska Peninsulas, and the Aleutian chain are warmed by the Japanese current and its associated warm air masses, which tend to moderate the weather in all those areas. Interior Alaska weather is another story altogether, as I was to find out.

I didn't settle in Anchorage. I settled in a little cabin high on a hill overlooking Lake Louise in south central interior Alaska. Fortunately, for most of my first winter the weather was mild. It was zero to ten below stuff, relatively easy to take. In fact I got letters from friends in Denver asking why I had shipped all the cold down there.

Then, late in the winter, I got a taste of what real cold is . . . .

If I had known the agonies of extreme cold I would have to endure that first winter in interior Alaska, I would most certainly have been scared off. I would never have come to Alaska. I didn't know it could get that cold anywhere.

This is looking north past the edge of my cabin and another old army cabin, identical to mine but without air space under its floor. It was extremely cold that day.

I didn't know that the cold was a creeping, live thing that defied everything I learned in all my high-school and college physics courses, which taught me that cold was just the simple absence of heat. Sorry, that's not the whole story. The cold is something tangible, something dreadfully dangerous. It can bite deep. It can torture or kill you.

The cold comes in the long nights of midwinter in interior Alaska. The cold comes, shyly at first, silently. It approaches softly and all grows still. Nothing is moving outside. You become gradually aware that it's very cold outside and growing colder. The temperature drops and drops. And keeps on dropping.

The cold comes, at first a deep chill that you can feel in your bones. With gathering strength it grows bolder and the temperature drops still more, more than you ever dreamed possible. The killing cold softly brushes the windows, taps at the door, rolls and creaks gently over the roof and 'round the chimney, beckoning silently. It settles in.

When the cold comes and climbs up your cabin wall and it finds the cracks between the logs and slips in silently to laugh at you and mock your feeble fire, when the cabin walls—logs dead for thirty years—creak and pop in agony as they cringe from the fifty-below cold, and when the wind comes as handmaiden to the cold and the wind howls across the lake and strikes hard on your cabin walls and shrieks at your windows and rushes off with your cloistered heat, then you will come to know that the cold is alive.

In your remote cabin there is no escape. No changing the channel. No second chance. Huddle close to your fire and hope you have enough food and fuel to last through the cold spell. The cold is alive and hungry. The cold is *here*!

The winters in south-central interior Alaska are generally colder than they are north of the Brooks range, on the North Slope. I have seen 70 degrees Fahrenheit below zero. (All temperatures mentioned in this book are in degrees Fahrenheit.) This happened one frigid night in February of '79, following two straight weeks of temperatures that never got warmer than 25 below zero.

My cabin stood on a hill some sixty feet above the surface of Lake Louise. Down on the lake surface it was significantly colder than up at the cabin. Down there on the lake it never got warmer than 35 below for three weeks. Day after day we had 40 to 50 below, and the climax of it all was the night the thermometer ran to the bottom of the scale at 68 below zero and kept on going. Here's what happened.

Jack Hansen, who then owned Evergreen Lodge, and I both had a similar system of temperature estimation that we checked every day against our thermometers. We would watch how high the frost line would get on a certain window in our respective dwellings. Every time it got to a certain point marked on our window frame, we knew it was 35 below, or 40 below, depending on how high the frost line got. The higher the frost line, the colder it was.

I had the temperature marked and written on the window frame and as the frost line got up to my calibration I could make a good guess of the temperature without having to go outside to read my thermometer. The thermometer was mounted on a tree about ten feet from the cabin. Every time I checked I found a very close correlation. Jack was doing the same thing at his place across the lake and he could also tell, within a few degrees, what the outside temperature was without reading the thermometer.

One crystal-clear night we were both alarmed to see our frost line indicators go so high that we had no idea how to interpret 'em. They hadn't ever been that high before. Jack checked his thermometer and it was pegged at minus 68 degrees F., so we conservatively estimated it had to be at least 70 below. I wasn't brave enough to go outside and check my thermometer!

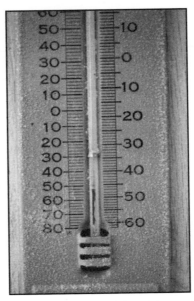

**During my first winter it got
even colder than 52 below.**

While the frost line would raise three inches from minus 20 to minus 30, and an additional two inches from minus 30 to minus 40, this time the frost line was a full six inches above the minus 40 mark, so I knew it was COLD!

The good news is that it didn't stay at minus 70 for long. By noon of the next day it was back up to a reasonable 40 below. (Incidentally minus 40 Fahrenheit is the same identical temperature as minus 40 Centigrade, the only temperature where the two coincide.)

That three-week cold spell was unusual in that it lasted so long and occurred so late in the winter. Temperatures had been around zero or slightly lower for the preceding two months, with an occasional excursion down to 20 below, once in a while up to 20 above. The following winter we had the really cold weather in late December and early January. The rest of the winter consisted of long months of temperatures hovering around zero. From time to time it would drop to minus 30 in January but only for a few days.

We had rain in January my second Alaskan winter, which was quite unusual. I'm told that we can expect a few days of severely cold weather every winter in interior Alaska. A week to ten days of 50- to 60-below temperatures every winter is the usual course of events. However, as I am writing this we're in the middle of a cold spell that's lasted more than two weeks and the temps have been near 60 below zero most of the time.

Last winter in late January I was trying to unstick my snowmobile from a snowdrift that was melting in the sun on an exceptionally warm day. It was nearly 60 degrees in the sun. It occurred to me that it was 120 degrees warmer than it had been a year before on the same date. You just never know.

My first Alaskan winter was marked by long weeks of incredibly still weather. There wasn't the slightest breath of wind most of the time, although when it did blow it made up for lost time. The weather was mostly mild until near the end of winter, and then the bottom dropped out of the thermometers as described above.

During my second Alaskan winter we had an almost predictable pattern of very cold spells followed by warmer days, snow, then high winds. Terrific winds came and blew all the new snow around into fantastic drifts. Then the pattern would repeat with another cold spell. Temperatures would drop and the new snowdrifts would get a thick crust on top. That pattern went on and on all winter.

I ran a trapline my second winter in Alaska, and had the loan of a snowmobile. The crusted snowdrifts made for lots of hard work on the trapline. When the snowmachine (that's what we northerners call a snowmobile) broke through the crust it got stuck. I had a hard time keeping the machine on the trail as I drove around my trapline. If I slid off the trail into the crusted snow next to it, I'd break through the crust and get stuck in the deep snow. Then I'd have to lift the 350-pound machine up out of the snow and back onto the trail before I could get going again. One gets lots of exercise running a trapline!

When I first arrived in Alaska I didn't have the slightest idea what was in store for me concerning the weather. The first order of business was to find a place to live, to be sure I could get out of the coming cold weather.

Just when I was about to give up hope I got lucky. My first Alaskan friend, the late Lennie Fitzpatrick, told me to look on "Army Point," where the army had built and later abandoned a group of cabins on a hill overlooking Lake Louise, not far from Lennie's home. Army Point was a recreational facility for army personnel in years long past. The army had built dozens of cabins, used them for a few years, and then abandoned them. Local residents had found better uses for the cabins than letting them rot on Army Point. They dragged some of them across the ice and tore down others for firewood. When I arrived on the scene there were only three cabins remaining in the area.

I picked what I thought was the best of the three cabins and moved in. It was not the most sound of the remaining cabins, nor the most level. However, it had the best roof and it also had some room under the floorboards that I could block off as dead-air space to help insulate the floor. It also had the best view of the lake. It turned out to be a good choice.

Two of the cabins on the top of the hill at Army Point, Lake Louise, Alaska. The cabin on the right with smokestack is mine. I picked what I thought was the best of three there.

Once I had found my cabin I went right to work to winterize it. It was then late fall, early October in fact. The cabin had a rudimentary door, nothing in the windows but air, big cracks in the walls between the logs, no furnishings whatsoever, and a slightly leaky roof.

I had a lot of work to do and winter was fast coming on. I had no idea of how much time I had before it got really cold, and frankly I was afraid of the cold. The coldest weather I had experienced at that time was 20 below, one frigid Colorado night. I had no practical experience with the cold and didn't know what to expect. I was dreading the first night I'd see 20 below in that cabin.

I made a good door, put Visqueen on all the walls and in the windows to keep the wind out, and worked hard to stockpile wood. I had a barrel stove that Lennie Fitzpatrick had made for me and I didn't know how well it worked. Fear of the unknown is one of the greatest fears of all, and I knew nothing of extreme cold, so I waited for the first really cold weather and worked with a vengeance.

One morning I awoke refreshed and looked out my little window at the beautiful view of Lake Louise. I was astonished at the perfect, clear view I had across the lake toward the Alaska range to the north. I had never seen those mountains before. I could see the distant mountains as though they were only a few miles off, just across the lake. They are actually about fifty miles away. I quickly set up my spotting scope outside and I was studying the surrounding wilderness when Lennie Fitzpatrick's boy, Lance, came by.

Lance asked me, "How did you sleep last night?"

"Perfectly well," I told him.

He told me it had been 34 degrees below zero the preceding night! It was in fact, right at that minute, 20 below zero. At first I didn't believe him. There I was with just a thin jacket on, enjoying the view! The thermometer proved him right, it was pretty cold out. So much for fear of the cold!

It was a tremendous relief to me to realize that I could cope with some of the most severe weather Alaska had to offer. Cold is relative, of course. I had been expecting to freeze solid the first time I went out in minus 30 weather, and that just doesn't happen. You get accustomed to the cold, and then when you get a warm spell it feels much warmer to your body than you would expect from reading the thermometer.

It happened that I first experienced really cold weather (30 below) after I had spent a month working long, hard hours outdoors every day. I had also been eating twice as much as I'd normally eat. I had become acclimatized to the cold without realizing it. I might add I was, at the time thirty-six years old. I looked like I was twenty. After a few years in the cold I came to look my age . . . at least.

You must be well prepared physically and mentally to be able to function in the Alaskan winters. Good health and well-being are the best defenses against extreme cold. You must also be physically clean and well-fed, and, of course, well dressed.

I found my cabin late in the fall. I needed to burn lots of wood right from the start because it got pretty chilly at night. I had not had time to gather any sort of long-term wood supply, so I was doomed to spend about two hours outside each and every day throughout the winter, gathering wood. By midwinter I was acclimatized enough that I was able to function outdoors while dressed quite lightly, even in very cold weather.

For example, one night I went to dine with Jack and Jan Hansen at their lodge (Evergreen), which was about a half mile walk across the lake ice from my cabin. When I put on my light "car coat" to go home, Jack and Jan couldn't believe that that was all I was wearing. They couldn't believe I would be warm enough with just that light jacket. I walked home in perfect comfort even though it was 38 below zero on the lake that night.

My coat was a common Dacron-insulated one that came down halfway to my knees. Under it I wore a wool shirt, and I had cotton long johns under my pants. I had a hat and light scarf, gloves, and that was it. I was perfectly comfortable for that short walk home, although I would not have liked to spend the night outdoors wearing only that amount of clothing. However, that was all I wore when I was out gathering firewood even when it was 50 below zero on the lake. I often had to take off my coat when it was 20 below and work in my shirtsleeves to avoid getting too hot.

My cabin was on top of a hill about sixty feet higher than the lake. It was on a peninsula of land that fell away to a bowl of spruce on the west, and dropped steeply downhill to the lake on the east. Lake Louise stretched to the north. The east slope was where I found all the standing dead wood (mostly birch) for my fire. To get wood I went down a path I had worn in the steep hillside, all the way down to the lake. Then I walked about 100 yards along the surface of the lake on a path I had trampled into the snow. Then I would climb halfway back up the hillside to a stand of dead timber, and I would knock down a few dead trees with the Swede saw, cut the trees into lengths I could pack on my shoulder, then pack them back downhill to the lake, retrace the 100 yards along my path there, and again up the steep hillside to the cabin.

My wood-hauling began in earnest the first day I spent on the lake. I got my timber by cutting standing dead trees and hauling them up the hill to the cabin. The vertical distance was about sixty-five feet, and the horizontal distance was anywhere from 50 to 200 yards, depending on where I found dead timber. Most of the wood was cut with a thirty-inch Swede saw, not the axe. I never used a chain saw.

**Chopping worked well, but I eventually found
sawing to be more practical and less tiring.**

Then I had to buck these logs into two-foot sections to fit in
the stove. About two or three hours of this a day would keep me in
firewood. I might add that all that exercise also paid long dividends
of top-notch health.

At night when I finished the daily woodcutting, the bottom of
my trousers would be stiff with ice. I'd hang 'em near the fire to
thaw and dry for the next day's chores. I never used a chain saw to
cut my firewood in all my time on Lake Louise. I never had a chain
saw, and had no snowmobile that first year. It was all manual labor
and shank's mare.

The daily woodcutting excursions were not without their
benefits. I have already mentioned the long-term advantages to my
health. Once in a while I met with some of my wild neighbors.

One day I found a little boreal owl (*Aegolius funereus*) roosting in a tree where I had been doing some woodcutting. I was surprised at the intensity of his yellow eyes, bright points of color in a drab winterscape. He could hardly keep them open and he seemed unable to see me clearly, even though it was broad daylight. He didn't seem afraid, and apparently had no intentions of leaving. I got my camera and took some photos of the little bird, who was only about eight inches long. I got my pictures and then I went to find my wood elsewhere, leaving him to his snooze.

A few nights later I went out to look at the northern lights. I stood on my front porch watching the lights dance on the stars. Suddenly out of the black of night something flashed past my head without a sound and landed on the tree next to me. I thought it was a bat, then I looked closer and saw it was the little owl, come to repay my visit. He set up residence near the cabin and did a good job of keeping the voles and shrews out of it. He took to roosting in the tree near my door. One day I went out to look at the thermometer and found myself face to face with the little owl, no more than two feet separating our beaks.

There was another benefit I was to realize from all my exertions by the end of winter. When I first started hauling wood up that hill it was all I could do to carry a few pathetic sticks up to the top, little things about three inches in diameter. I would drop them in a heap by the door, then crawl inside and lie down to rest. I was completely exhausted from all the hard work, more than I had done in years. I was very much out of shape when I first started these exertions: the result of years of relatively no significant exercise.

I would rest a while, then go out and cut up the twigs to fit the stove, then back inside to rest some more. I remember the first time I was able to bring up the sticks and cut them up without resting between jobs, and it was a landmark in my reconditioning. As the winter wore on I gradually became stronger. One day I found myself carrying logs up that hill I never even dreamed I could lift. My daily investment in "exercise" had paid vast dividends of increased strength and health.

Fighting the weather gets you nowhere. You'll get used to the cold if you learn to live with the conditions in Alaska, not against them. You'll soon learn to dress and eat to match the weather if you listen to what your body says. You'll come to crave fats and you'll eat lots of food, and you won't gain weight except as muscle. You'll breathe some of the cleanest air left in the world and drink some of the cleanest water, right out of the lake or stream. Once you have come to grips with Alaska's cold, you'll thrive in every way in a manner most gratifying to yourself.

HOW TO DRESS

The following is a description of how I dressed for cold weather during my second winter in Alaska, when I was not burdened with hauling wood. I ran a trapline instead, which was very hard work even though I rode a snowmobile all day. The work was in getting it unstuck!

First, I wore the same lightweight cotton underwear that I have worn all my life. Over this went a two-piece suit of cotton thermal long underwear. I then put on one or two pair of pure wool socks. Then I wore Levis, though I have come to prefer slacks of some sort, trousers loose enough to let me move inside them, and not so long as to reach the ground.

I wore pure wool shirts, and the only problem I had with them was getting them large enough so I could still wear them after some well-intentioned idiot washed them and then dried them in a hot clothes dryer. (Mebbe I oughta say fried, not dried!) An acquaintance who claimed to know all about wool shirts got hold of several of my best Pendletons and shrank them so they were completely useless.

I mentioned Pendletons and I must comment about them. Many years before I came to Alaska I wore Pendleton shirts and they gave good service. That was *long* ago. When I lived in my little cabin at Lake Louise I never had an abundance of money, to put it politely. One day when I had saved some money from trapping I went to town to get a new shirt. I bought a beautiful new Pendleton. It cost over $40 at the time, about what I was getting for a good marten hide. A few days later while tucking it into my pants I put my thumb through my new shirt. It went through easily, the material being of very low quality. I was, and still am, furious with that company for producing such a shoddy piece of goods.

This is a marten, one of the more mysterious north-woods critters, in that not too much is known about them. They are a ferocious predator, pound for pound as savage as any grizzly.

That shirt proceeded to fall to rags in the next few weeks, though I never abused it. The elbows split the first time I bent my arms, and on and on. Unless Pendleton have totally changed their methods and their suppliers I can't recommend them. I was so poor then I couldn't even afford a letter to complain about it, much less return to town to exchange the shirt.

Be sure your clothing is not tight-fitting. Get your clothes cut loose and "fashion" be damned. Leave all notions of "fashion" behind you in the city. You will only look and feel like a fool in the bush wearing tight duds.

I had some army surplus black insulated rubber boots that worked very well. Most of the time they were entirely adequate, especially if I was able to move around a little and build up some circulation. Lots of folks who live in the bush wear the so-called "bunny-boot," which is similar to what I had, but better insulated and white instead of black. They are the most ungainly-looking clodhoppers I have ever seen, but apparently they work extremely well. Everyone who has used them seems to be happy with them. They are apparently a military development. My friend, the late Harry Billum, used them on his 400-mile (yes, four-hundred-mile) trapline and had no complaints. He was out from before dawn to well after dusk just about every day in winter and he spent many a night out, sleeping along the trail by his snowmachine, a pretty good test of winter duds.

That was the basic set of clothes I wore every day in winter, indoors or out. When I ventured outdoors I would add to it as follows: a down vest, a snowsuit (a one piece garment with zippers, sort of a coverall with insulation), and, if it was really cold, my Dacron-insulated car coat on top of everything. A parka would have been better, but I didn't own one. Snowsuits are available in a wide variety of protection ranges and styles and are sold in the major trade centers throughout Alaska, and at snowmobile dealers. Carhartts are the standard all over Alaska. Prices at the time were from $60–$150. A good parka would have cost $100–$250, depending on the type and amount of insulation.

For headgear I wore a wool stretch pullover that covered my entire head and left only a hole for nose and eyes. On top of that went another wool cap, the "tuque" or common watch cap. When I went around my trapline on the snowmachine I wore a good pair of goggles, the non-fogging kind with two panels of Plexiglas.

Goggles or face shields are mandatory for snowmobile use, whether or not your snow-go has a windshield.

One day a greenhorn from Anchorage came to Lake Louise with his buddies to spend the weekend doing some high-speed touring with snowmobiles. It was a frosty 40 below. You can't feel the cold when it gets that low because there's no moisture in the air. There is a diminished sensation of freezing, with none of the pain associated with freezing more gradually.

This poor joker decided to freeze-dry his face. He thought he could get by with no goggles or face mask of any sort. Imagine the chill factor from the combination of 40 below temperatures and an induced breeze of 60 miles per hour!

I helped swab that joker's face and neck later that day after he came in from his high-speed ramble across the lake. We managed to save some of his hide. His face and neck were as red as a boiled beet. He says, "I didn't think it was that cold!" His first three words said it all.

If I knew that I was going to be out on a snowmachine all day I would strap my heaviest coat onto the back of the snowmachine. If the snowmachine had a breakdown, the heavy coat was a handy friend. Of course I also had fire makin's.

When I was running a trapline I always had along my old Smith & Wesson K-22 sixgun, riding in a Bianchi shoulder holster. I hung the gun next to the fire at night and then I'd have a warm chunk of iron under my arm in the morning, not a chunk of ice. That helped keep me warm every day for a short time, before the cold got to the gun.

I bought a pair of army surplus wool mittens in Anchorage at a surplus store for four dollars. Over these I wore a pair of deer-hide mittens I stitched up from a piece of tanned, western-Montana mule deer hide that I brought up to Alaska. I used dental floss for the stitching. Dental floss is a good substitute for moose sinew, the traditional thread used by natives. These two layers of material, the wool and the leather, kept my hands warm even when the mittens were soaked with water, no matter how cold it got.

I have seen similar but heavier mittens that have extensions up your arm like a gauntlet, military surplus items, I believe. I think the extensions up your arm are a good idea if you're going to spend any time on a snowmachine. Some of these gauntlets are sold with wool liners which, like all wool, will keep you warm even when wet. Gloves won't do the job. You need to keep your fingers together to help generate warmth, and this means mittens.

It's a good idea to avoid sweating while working outdoors in the winter. If you sweat, you lose a lot of body heat as the sweat evaporates. You may not even be aware of it until some time later, when you feel cold even though you have an abundance of clothes.

"What's wrong?" you'll say. "This kept me warm this morning!" You may be unaware you're getting cold until it's too late and hypothermia sets in.

When I was breaking trail out on the trapline I fought the snowmobile tooth and nail. I was often running sweat. I'd get unstuck and then a little ways down the trail I'd start to shiver. Several times I knew I should have turned back and taken the easy way home, but instead I plugged doggedly onward until I noticed I was doing stupid things. I was in the early stages of hypothermia, and lucky to realize it. It was time to turn the nose of old "Black Jack" (my snowmobile) toward the home fires.

When I got home in that condition it would take a couple of hours in front of the fire and (if I was extremely lucky!) a big bowl of Ruthie Runyan's fine chili before I'd stop shaking. If I had had a breakdown on the trail, the first order of the day would have been to build a fire. I always carried fire makin's on the trail: matches, tinder, candle, and a lighter, several good ways to get a flame and keep it burning.

Nowhere in this book do I want to give the impression that wintering in interior Alaska is a piece of cake. Nothing could be farther from the truth. The cold will kill you if you let it. Boiled down this means: If your fire goes out, you die.

Before you get through your first winter in Alaska you'll cuss yourself, me, and anyone else you can think of for ever leaving hearth and home in the warm south. You'll get sick and tired of cold and more cold. You'll hope against hope that the next time you go outside you won't feel the chill in your bones and it'll be warm, the snow starting to melt, the birds singing, the sun shining. Yet when you open the door it's still dark and cold, still snowing, day after day, week after week, and it looks like it'll go on forever. You'll probably get very depressed your first winter, and you'll promise on your great-grandfather's grave you'll never spend another winter in Alaska.

Winter finally hit and brought the deep snow. The car is well-buried. Jack Hansen came from Evergreen Lodge a couple of times and plowed me a road, but then the snow got too deep, so I kept my car at the lodge. I made only five or six trips to town all winter.

I did all this and more. Yet I spent the next two winters in the Alaskan bush. I discovered that I was actually looking forward to the cold weather as a relief from the brief hot summer.

Your second winter will be much better, much easier than the first. You'll have a lot of the doubt and trauma overcome and you'll have a feeling for the rhythm of the north. You'll start to fit in. Still, along about March you'll start to ask yourself, "Will this winter ever end?" and you still have two months of cold and snow in front of you. The long cold winters of the far north are not for everyone. Many newcomers spend only one winter in the Alaskan bush and then choose to spend their time in southern, warmer, climates. Cold weather is the reason Alaska has a low population and always will. Today, with little work to be had throughout the state, the population of Alaska is actually diminishing.

A final note on cold weather. If you're mentally prepared to dominate the cold, you will. Otherwise, stay home. Nothing, no clothing, equipment, or anything you can buy can substitute for the positive mental attitude that you'll need in the winter in Alaska.

Tools

Some come to Alaska to build their own home. Some come to move into an already built structure. No matter which you choose, you will need tools. You'll want to modify any existing structure, count on it. You won't be happy unless you have a complete set of hand tools for various jobs. By hand tools I mean those that work without electricity. If you decide to have an auxiliary generator you'll want a few power tools as well. Tools can include guns, and they're important enough that I cover them in a separate chapter. Keep in mind the basics of food, clothing, and shelter as you select your tools, and be sure to select them so they will help you to be able to provide, make, or repair these basics.

Be sure you have all the hand-powered tools you need as a basic set. If all else fails, if you can't get gasoline or fuel oil, you can still do all the necessary work and repairs of day-to-day living if you have equipment that requires only the power that you provide with your own hands. It is really nice to have gasoline-powered ice augers, snowmobiles, and even a portable generator. In fact, if transportation is no problem, I recommend a generator and power tools to relieve the burden of coping with Alaskan conditions.

However, I think it's unwise to count on the uninterrupted re-supply of energy sources to run your power tools—diesel fuel, gasoline, oil, etc. In the deep bush of Alaska you never know when fuel supplies will run out. In fact we have already seen the results of social disorder in the Los Angeles riots of a few years ago, and of course the mess in New Orleans from the floods. Plan for no fuel and be happy when you can get any at all.

In short, buy the brace and bit before you buy the electric drill and generator. Buy the snowshoes before the snowmobile. Get an ice chipper before you buy the power ice auger. And put in a good supply of firewood before you run out of fuel oil.

When I arrived in Alaska I was lucky to find a deserted cabin in which to live, but it needed lots of work. Fortunately there was also a good supply of available scrap lumber that I could use to improve my cabin. I had no electric power source but I did have good hand carpenter tools.

The cabin and I as I first knew it, my first week in there. Note the open ceiling, cracks in the walls, a rough bench, and just a few shelves on the walls.

Cabin interior, looking the other way toward the poor door that just barely covers the entry. That's my first barrel stove, the one Lennie Fitzpatrick made for me. One of my first jobs was to make a better cabin door.

Most of the wood I had to work with had already been used, and I pulled lots of nails. I wished many times for a good nail-puller. A wrecking bar would have been handy. At times, a wrecking crew would have been handy! I broke the wood handle on my favorite hammer; I recommend steel-handled hammers, or the ones with the new synthetic handles. I also used a hand sledge for heavy pounding, and could have used a full-size sledgehammer more than once.

I had a good carpenter's saw, which I used for the finish work, those neat jobs that I would see and use often, such as on the cupboards and the like. For rough work, cutting timbers for the porch floor, notching logs, and, most important, cutting firewood, my most valuable tool was a good Swede saw, or bow saw as they are sometimes called. I had a Sears brand with a thirty-inch blade. I chose the length by measuring the distance my arm moved in a sawing motion. I wanted just enough blade length so that I could use full strokes of my arm, not so long that the saw would be clumsy or too heavy, and not so short that my sawing efforts would be so much nervous scratching. The thirty-inch length was perfect for me.

The Sears Craftsman saw turned out to be an extremely well-made and solid piece of goods. There were times in the dead of winter that I would not have taken $1,000 for that saw, even though it cost only around $8.

Get a half dozen extra blades for your saw. They're not brittle, just hard to replace when you're 200 miles from town, back in the bush. In fact this is a good thing to keep in mind about all your tools and other equipment. Not only may it be impossible to replace certain items, due to their being no longer available anywhere; but also, even if they are available you may not be able to get to town to replace them because of weather conditions or some other crisis. A harsh environment imposes its own sort of "national crisis."

A good hacksaw with an assortment of blades is a fine tool to have handy.

A medium or small hand plane will come in handy for rounding and smoothing wood edges. This keeps splinters to a minimum. I used mine often and I liked it better than sandpaper. It was faster and equally good for most jobs. Bring a good supply of sandpaper, though, with emphasis on the coarser grades for wood. I like the wet-or-dry types for finish woodworking.

A drawknife is good to have if you plan to work with logs. They slice off the bark and leave a smooth peeled log. Good exercise, these. That's a hint!

Other tools you'll find necessary are good C-clamps (about a half dozen medium and one or two big ones), pliers (Channel-locks and ordinary), a good small Crescent wrench, wire cutters (for chrissakes, get some *good* ones!), a good assortment of wood screws, some nails of assorted sizes, a good axe, files, a rasp, and a good brace and an assortment of bits.

A good hand drill and a set of small high-speed steel (HSS) drill bits in number sizes, or by sixteenths from 1/16 to 1/2 inch, will be very useful. The HSS drill bits are expensive, but well worth the cost.

I had an old but still serviceable hand-powered eggbeater-type hand drill to spin the bits, and it was a much-used item.

A brace & bit was one of the tools I left behind and greatly regretted not having, as a good set of hand-driven augers would many times have done me good service. I also could have used a good big wood chisel. If you contemplate log work, one of the huge slick chisels of about three inches' width is a good tool to have. I left behind a fairly large best-quality Wilton bench vise that I wished many times I had brought along. I just couldn't find room in the car for it.

For simple wood finishing it's hard to beat linseed oil. A gallon will go a long way.

KNIVES

Don't forget an assortment of sharpening stones and a sharpening steel. I assume you'll bring a good selection of knives. Anyone going anywhere in the bush away from the beaten path ought to carry some sort of knife. Surely that is common sense, but to what uses might you want to put that blade? Cleaning small game or cutting off an offending small branch, maybe making a feather stick to start a fire, things like that are examples of the prime uses for such a tool. Back at the cabin you'll use your knife to case out any critters you have trapped. In my experience a knife that stays razor-sharp a long time, particularly in trapping work, is superior to one that won't rust. Therefore I chose carbon-steel for my most-used blades. You might want a specialized fish knife. Unless you plan to settle in an area of extreme alders, such as Kodiak Island, I think you'll find a machete to be useless, though a folding saw like the excellent Bahco Laplander or the faster-cutting Silky Gomboy will be mighty handy.

The huge knives that Rambo and Crocodile Dundee carried have no real use in Alaska, other than as objects for animated discussion around the campfire. Katanas are in the same category. I never carried a belt knife. For years I used a small Buck "Personal" knife for all my hunting, but I didn't take it to Alaska. I carried a small folding pocket knife by Schrade (Parker-Frost), called the Mink, with two slim blades, three inches long, made of carbon steel. It served for all small game, trapping, and even to open up a caribou. In short, it was all the outdoors-use knife I needed. Diligent care kept the carbon-steel blades from rusting. I also had a fine skinner by Marbles, with a five-inch curved blade, and I used it once to cape out a big caribou head. I also had a small folding knife about three inches long that fit in a belt sheath, with a curved blade. I used it a time or two, but I valued it too highly to ever carry, because it was scrimshawed by Andy Runyan with an image of my cabin on Army Point.

Andy Runyan on his trapline. Trapping is a way of life in the north, and it makes the winter fly past. Nothing I have done in my life has been harder work than trapping, but nothing else made the winter pass more quickly. A task such as trapping is a good way to keep one's sanity during the long winter. The late Mr. Runyan was a Master Guide, probably the best guide in Alaska for Kodiak bear and caribou, and also a pretty good wolf trapper.

Folding blades with locks are handy, and are easier to carry than a fixed-blade. There are thousands of them available. I don't believe you'll ever need a blade longer than five inches. By all means, get a good one. For kitchen usage stainless knives are probably better, but the carbon-steel ones hold a better edge and hold it longer. Your choice.

ADDITIONAL EQUIPMENT

For several years I was a professional gunsmith and I still do some considerable tinkering with my own firearms, so I brought a tool chest of gun-working tools along. I put them to use on many jobs besides fiddling with my firearms. If you're an avid woodworker or metalsmith or other specific hobbyist, you'll undoubtedly have some tools that you'll find indispensable anywhere in the world that you happen to find yourself; so it was with my gun tools. I can't tell you every single item you'll need or want in the line of tools. The ones I have mentioned are those most likely to be used.

I brought some tools almost grudgingly, that I thought I would never have needed at all. For instance, I bought my Sears Swede saw almost as an afterthought and had to do some hard searching before I found just what I wanted. I nearly left it in the store. I would have had to make do with just an axe. Something told me to get it, and of course I never regretted it.

Get top-quality goods for all survival and retreat use. I can't emphasize this enough. Cheaper items look okay when you compare prices, but a bargain that falls apart after a little use is the worst kind of false economy, and doubly so when it is impossible to replace. I repeat: Don't buy cheap tools!

Some lengths of good stout rope are indispensable. You'll find many uses for ropes, so bring a good assortment: clothesline size up to good stout half-inch stuff, or even larger. Also, some parachute cord or thin nylon line will come in mighty handy.

Bring needles and thread, and make sure the thread is nylon, not cotton. Also get a couple of leather needles, the kind with a triangular point. If you want to make a pair of mittens, as I did, bring some leather with you. You can use dental floss for sewing. It is extremely strong, and a good substitute for moose sinew, the traditional sewing thread. You'll find commercially tanned leather easier to work with than untanned caribou hides. It is possible to tan your own leather, but I preferred to use some Montana mule deer hides I had tanned. There are some patent stitching awls available, but I have no experience with them. What I had worked very well.

If you're shaky on any aspect of woods lore such as leather-working, woodworking, care of tools, cooking, etc., there are many good handbooks on these subjects available at your bookstore. Get the books and include them in your library. Read them before you come up to get an idea of what special tools you might need for these craft items that you maybe haven't considered. One of the better books is the *Boy Scout Handbook*.

Take a camping trip and try out that new Swede saw. Can you really put a good edge on your knife or axe? Try making a bench or table from some logs and see what tools you need that you don't have. Make a list. Check it twice. Even if it's naughty . . . or nice.

If someone in your family is inclined toward knitting, don't neglect this aspect of clothing manufacture. Wool is best. Get used to it.

THINGS I NEVER THOUGHT OF:

- An ice spud, which can be just an old axe head securely welded to a stout pipe with a cord on the other end. The ice spud is used to chip your way through the ice on the lake to get water, and for making holes for ice fishing. You wrap the cord around your wrist so that when your chipper goes through the last of the ice you won't lose it.
- A big scoop with holes to scoop out the ice from the water hole before filling your buckets. This simple tool will keep most of the ice chunks out of your water.
- Buckets. You did remember to bring a trio of buckets, didn't you? Two five-gallon buckets and a normal two-gallon bucket (not flimsy plastic!) are the minimums. You may want a jerry can or two for hauling water, but the two big buckets work well.

I used brand-new plastic gasoline containers that I washed thoroughly and labeled "For water use only."
- Two wash basins, one for hands and one for dishes. Keep them separate.
- A new (unused) large clean plastic garbage can for water storage . . . twenty or thirty gallons per can. If you want, you can add a bit of Clorox bleach to disinfect the water, or even water purification tablets. I drank what I dipped, straight from the lake, and never suffered from it.

OTHER BITS & PIECES

You may want an assortment of small hinges for cupboard doors, etc.

Bring larger-than-normal cooking utensils. You won't believe how much you eat when you're spending lots of time outdoors.

Cross-country skis are useful and popular items for many Alaskans, though I have little use for them. In other circumstances, though, I can see where they could be mighty handy, or even essential. Depends on where you settle and the surrounding terrain. They provide excellent exercise (a) if you are not running a trapline or (b) if you need more exercise than you'll normally get thrashing out your daily living in the north. Running a trapline was the hardest, most bone-racking work I've ever done in my life. I sure didn't need cross-country skis for more exercise.

If you can use them, a set of acetylene welding torches are extremely useful for repairs and for making tools.

The first sort of power tool to buy ought to be a good snowmobile with a drag-along sled of some kind. The snowmobile, usually called a snowmachine, is one of the most useful tools in the north. Much of today's snowmachine advertising emphasizes speed and power. Power is mandatory, speed is not. Knowledgeable Alaskans who rely on their snowmachines as working tools six or more months a year will often get a hot-rod machine and gear it down so they can go slow and haul a good load. You don't need a 100 mph machine.

If you run a trapline on a snowmachine you'll putt along all day at an average speed of about seven miles an hour. If you run a trapline on a snowmachine, you'll probably need at least two machines, one to continue running the line while the other is down for repairs. If you gear down a good machine you'll be able to ride a long distance at low speed without burning up your drive belt. Drive belts are expensive and spares are sometimes hard to get. Some of the newest breed of snowmachines are designed with utility in mind more than speed, and they have such nice things as very long tracks that float better in deep snow, and are already geared down. When you buy your snowmobile, be sure you can get parts for it easily and that spare-part distribution is compatible with your needs. If in doubt, ask which brands of snowmobiles are the most common in the area where you intend to settle, because snowmachine brand preferences are definitely provincial.

Other recommended power tools are a good chain saw, an ice auger, and a little portable generator of around two to five kilowatts. Most of the small generators run on gasoline. The little generators are really nice. All you need to do to get electricity is tug lightly on the starting cord and then flip a switch. The little Honda 2KW weighs something like 100 pounds and will run a power saw or hand drill or radio or (am I nuts?) a computer, with good gasoline economy. When I was in Alaska the Internet didn't exist. Today, I have no idea what you can link to in the bush, but really, what's the point? A shortwave radio would be lots more useful, seems to me.

A citizens-band radio might be handy if you're in a community that uses them in place of telephones, as the Lake Louise community used to. I used a car battery for power, and I recharged the battery simply by running the car engine on a drive to town. The hot setup today is to use solar panels to recharge whatever batteries you happen to use.

In some areas, especially those most remote from the passways of man, you might want a good two-way radio to communicate your emergency needs. Along the same lines, a good shortwave receiver will let you find out what is really going on throughout the world, if you're interested. Some shortwave stations broadcast really good news stuff, items that you never hear on the very biased and edited "mainstream" TV and radio stations. If you have never listened to shortwave news broadcasts it'll amaze you the first time you hear some of the real news of the world, news that Peter Jennings, Dan Rather, Brian Williams, and Walter Cronkite never told you, let alone your favorite talking head today.

Much, if not all, of the news we hear on American TV and radio stations is edited so that it is less scary. It is closer to entertainment than to news. (Mustn't alarm the peasants, you know.) If you don't believe me, listen to the news out of Britain or some other English-language news broadcasts on shortwave stations, and then compare what you heard there with what your favorite mainstream talking head tells you on the six o'clock news. I, too, was a skeptic until I tried this. We are not given the whole story, or even a significant part of it in many cases. We are instead given entertainment, lies, and even government propaganda in the name of news.

In any kind of retreat situation I think it's a bad idea to rely on power tools to do your work. There may come a time when all your energy sources run out. (See above on solar panels. Many items such as lights, radios, and kitchen accessories are available with twelve-volt options, and solar panels are getting cheaper and more efficient with each passing year.) Power tools are dandy when you have lots of fuel, but given the difficulties of obtaining gas in remote areas, and the overall trend of fossil fuels becoming scarcer or more costly to extract at any price, it's good practice to learn how to use hand-powered tools. I've found it's often a lot quicker and sometimes even better to use a hand tool than any sort of electrically powered device, and it can be far more satisfying. I recall the great simplicity of using a small hand plane to bevel the edges of the wood things I made in the cabin, and still use such a tool today frequently in my wood shop instead of breaking out a router. Hand tools are generally easy to learn how to use, but you might want someone to show you some tricky things like how to set a blade in a hand plane. Try out your tools before you head north.

At least part of the idea behind a retreat is to have a place to go when social disorder becomes the norm, and I personally would spend additional money on insulation and good food stores against such emergencies than on power equipment. However, there are those who must have power, whether for health reasons or whatever, and it then becomes prudent to think about very large tanks to store gasoline and fuel oil.

Big fuel tanks will make you a big target for looters if they find out about your energy stores. How to hide the tanks? In much of Alaska you can't just bury these tanks, because if you go through permafrost your tanks might sink, and keep on sinking. It would take a mighty good fuel pump to draw fuel up from China. Clever camouflage might work.

GETTING WATER

Many folks who want to retreat to Alaska have never had to get water out of a frozen lake. How do you do it? It's not very difficult once you know how, but there are some tricks. Here's how to do it, in detail.

Let us assume you are on a lake in central Alaska, it is midwinter and you need water. The lake is covered with three or four feet of ice. The main thing to keep in mind is that once you chop through the last bit of ice and hit water, the water will come right up to the top of your lovely ice hole and fill it full. It is very difficult to chip ice under water, so you better have most of the ice chipped out of the way before any of it gets wet.

Start chipping a hole about two or three feet in diameter with your spud. (I assume you don't have a power ice auger.) Let the weight of the chipper do most of the work and remove the loose ice as you go down. When you get near the bottom, just before you think you are going to break through, make sure the hole is smoothed up pretty good on the sides, and then take the hole down evenly around the edges. You can leave a hump of ice in the center of the bottom, and when you have chipped through to water all around, you can shove the hump, or plug, down through the hole and it will come up against the ice underneath and be out of the way. *Voilá!* You have a water supply.

In order to keep your water supply from freezing solid overnight, cover the hole with a piece of plywood and pile snow on top. The snow acts as an insulator and keeps the hole in good shape for quite a while, depending on air temperature and depth of snow. If you can pile about a foot of snow on top of the hole, and if there is a corresponding thickness of snow on top of the ice all around the hole, you ought to have easy water access for up to a week at air temperatures of 20 below. If you don't cover the hole it will freeze solid overnight. There aren't any rules about this, because much depends on how cold it has been the last few days and how cold the surrounding ice is. The hole will freeze from the surrounding ice in, no matter what you do. But the hole will freeze much faster from the colder air on top of the lake if you don't put a cover on it.

It's possible to shoot a hole in the ice. I spent many hours and fired many rounds of ammo experimenting with this idea. Any good centerfire rifle bullet will make lots of powdered ice with each shot. Good stout bullets like the Nosler work better than cheap, poorly-constructed, or thin-jacketed rifle slugs, same as they do in big game. Bigger rifles work much better than smaller ones, no matter the velocity. (Just like they do on big game, pilgrim!)

A 44 Mag sixgun firing Elmer Keith's cast bullet load works just about as well as a high-powered rifle. (I compared the Keith sixgun load with results from my 338 OKH, a wildcat much more powerful than the 30-06, and the handgun did about as well as the rifle.) The big cast pistol bullets stay in one piece, more than can be said for most rifle slugs I've tried. In fact, the 44 Mag is better than the rifle for chipping off a little ice below the surface of the water. The sixgun slug penetrates better and delivers a better smash to wet ice some six inches below the surface. Steel jacketed "solids" from a rifle go through lots of ice and keep on going, doing little damage to wet ice. They just punch a small hole.

One word of caution: a lot of water splashes up when you're engaged in such shenanigans, and some of it will get inside your rifle barrel. It'll immediately turn to ice, and you must bring your rifle indoors to dry the barrel between shots. If you don't dry your barrel you are likely to destroy your rifle. Oh sure, you can get killed too, but why destroy a good rifle in the process? Also note that low-powered pistol bullets can ricochet back into your face from "rubbery" ice. Be extremely careful shooting into ice!

The best results I got busting ice with ordnance was using 500-grain, paper-patched cast-lead slugs at about 2,100 feet per second out of my Churchill double 470, which is an elephant rifle. Man, did the ice fly!

The Cabin

My little cabin measured twelve by sixteen feet, and I spent three winters in it in reasonable comfort. There was enough room for me and everything I brought along. In fact, it was almost too much room for minimal survival conditions. If I did it again today, though, I'd get a larger cabin, especially if I were going to live there for more than a year or two. I would need additional storage space for the extra equipment and tools that, as I have found through experience, make life easier in the Alaskan bush.

I would build my cabin about fifteen by twenty feet, and I'd make sure it had at least two rooms. That would let me close off one room if I wanted to, and heat just half the cabin. This could be useful if I got sick or injured in the middle of winter, and couldn't gather enough wood to heat all the available space.

For two people, a cabin about twenty by twenty feet should be big enough; correspondingly larger with children in the family. The kids can help haul the extra wood you'll need to heat a bigger cabin.

There is really no big problem with having a large cabin provided you have adequate supplies of firewood or heating oil and top-quality insulation. However, you might want to—or have to—live there for many years, and the smaller the cabin the less work and expense needed to heat and insulate it. Remember, you spend a lot of time indoors during the six-to-eight-month-long winter. Build yourself some comfort. Cabin fever is no fun. That depressed condition comes to nearly every northern cabin dweller toward the end of winter when they've had too much darkness and inactivity.

Be sure to build an arctic entry to your cabin. This is a small room into which you enter from outdoors, big enough to let you remove your cold-weather gear and store it there. This saves lots of heat every time you go into or out of your cabin.

Don't build your ceiling any higher than necessary. Unless you have tons of insulation and a circulation fan you'll always have hot ceilings and cold floors to some extent. If the ceiling is too high you lose energy by having to heat your home too much, the heat going up and out the roof. About six inches' height over the tallest person's head ought to be plenty. In fact, you only need this height in the center of the cabin. I have seen a cabin that had the roof six feet high in the center, and it sloped to walls that were only four feet tall. Such an arrangement, while possibly claustrophobic for some, is easily heated.

I like to sit and stare out the window, and I probably do more of that than I ought to. If I built a cabin today I'd have the bottom of the windows low enough so I could easily see out when I was seated in my favorite easy chair. My old cabin sat high on a hill. The cabin floor was about three feet above the ground. The bottom of my favorite window was therefore well above the highest snowdrifts, and I had a great view of the surrounding lake country. It wouldn't have been much fun spending my winters staring at the inside of a snowdrift.

My cabin was made of logs that had been cut flat on three sides, the walls about four to five inches thick. The logs were warped and there were big gaps between layers of logs. I was unable to chink the gaps adequately because I didn't have enough time or materials. It was a cold and not very attractive cabin, and if I were building one now I would build it of round logs.

You can cut and peel your logs yourself, which is an enormous job, or in some areas you can buy them ready to go and have them delivered to your building site. If you plan to peel them yourself the usual method is to cut green logs, lay them up so air can circulate, let them dry for six months or so, and then peel off the bark. The bark separates from the core wood and is easier to get off. You now have clean, dry logs.

You can buy commercially peeled logs all ready to go, and this is what I'd do if I had my druthers. My druthers might come out to be pretty expensive, though.

I have seen commercially milled logs that are basically round, but they have a tongue and groove milled into the wood on top and bottom. These deserve a good look, but I suspect they will be costly. They also have much of the natural structure of the log opened up to moisture, which will shorten the life of your cabin unless the logs are very well preserved. Water gets into open grain far easier than it can penetrate through the natural outside of a peeled log, and wet wood spells rotten wood.

If you build with logs you will have bumpy walls. The logs may provide enough insulation, but I think you will be warmer and happier with some good commercial insulation inside the cabin. This can be laid between two-by-fours or two-by-sixes tacked to your walls, which you then cover with paneling. The layers of logs, air, insulation, and inner paneling will give you flat interior walls and very good insulation. Be sure to use a vapor barrier of Visqueen in the walls. Of course you can also go with typical framed-up construction, but the transportation costs might make that a poor second choice. Don't neglect floor insulation. The most comfortable cabin I have been in had ten inches of insulation under the floor.

Give some serious thought to under-floor storage. Whatever-you-can-think-of can be nicely out of the way stashed under the floor, yet be readily available when you need it.

You can also dig a hole under your floorboards. I saw a cabin that had a hole dug straight down under the floor about ten feet deep. The owner used it as a cold cellar for storage of perishables.

It didn't get cold enough to freeze and it kept his beer cold. He kept his stored items in a bucket on a rope, and when he wanted a cold brew all he had to do is open the trapdoor and haul up the bucket. He told me the temperature stayed at about 40 degrees all year long.

Much of Alaska is permafrost, which is permanently frozen ground with a natural insulation barrier of moss and lichen over it. This ought not to be disturbed when you build. The recommended method to build on top of permafrost is to build simple pads of heavy timbers (railroad ties) at the corners, resting them right on top of the permafrost/tundra. Several other pads here and there under the center of the floor area complete the foundation. You lay beams across the pads, and the floor joists rest on top of that. The bottom of that kind of structure, i.e., the area underneath the floor, has to be left open so the permafrost never melts from the heat of the dwelling above it. A double floor will give you space for insulation. A cabin built on permafrost may shift over time, with the result that it will sag here and there. When that happens, you shim the corners as needed to keep your cabin level. This is better than having your cabin sink into the ice of the permafrost, as it will if you disturb the insulating moss and lichen ground cover any more than you do with these simple pads.

There is another method used where the ground permits, which means where there is no permafrost. You sink a pipe about eight or nine inches in diameter down into the ground and fill it with concrete, then build on top of these plugs.

I love looking at trees, either live ones outside or logs in my ceiling. Accordingly, for my cabin roof I'd opt for an open log beam roof, consisting of a ridgepole and two parallel beams. These are overlaid with either a pole log roof or a frame construction roof. The main supporting beams are left open to the inside of the cabin. These open beams provide a nice effect and are great for hanging things. You just drive in a nail when you want to hang something. You don't have to diddle around with poking a hole in some plasterboard and then installing some trick screw that you hope will actually hold whatever it is you are trying to suspend, and if the darned thing doesn't work it brings half the ceiling down around your ears. Log beams make simply grand suspenders. If you want a really nice-looking job you can bore a hole with your auger and stick in a dowel or whittled peg for the hanging job. For looks and convenience I like the open beams on the ceiling. However, you'll have to have really good insulation above that, so it might make things somewhat complicated.

Pole roofs, the carefully matched set of sticks that form the actual roof, are stunningly good-looking if a bit impractical. I have seen a few of these, and they are truly gorgeous. However, such a roof can be a bit on the dark side, something to consider when planning your reading area.

I have seen many an Alaskan cabin with grass growing on the roof. While sod is available in many places throughout the state, I can't imagine dirt to be a better insulator than top-quality commercial fiberglass batting, or good, thick foam of some sort. Dirt is also heavier than conventional construction and adds weight to heavy snow loads.

Perhaps the simplest way to put a roof on a cabin is to first put a flat ceiling on the cabin, put the insulation on top of the ceiling, and then use trusses to form a gable over everything. The trusses are set every two feet. The trusses come either pre-built or are assembled on the spot. You stand them up along the roof and then cover them with corrugated metal sheeting. Such a roof insulates only by providing a dead air space over a subceiling or other insulation underneath. Tin roofs can look very good and are practically maintenance-free.

There are some very good books on cabin construction on the market. This is not intended to be one of them. I suggest you get one or several, and study what you find in them. They'll surely give you some good ideas concerning the best ways to put a top on your cabin, as well as many other construction kinks that I simply can't cover here. I'm sure you'll find something better for your roof than sod!

Frame construction is as common as cold weather in Alaska. All too common in frame-constructed cabins are walls that are too doggoned thin. You need about six inches of insulation in the walls, and about ten inches in the floors and ceiling. I doubt you can have too much insulation, but some bright engineer out there will have a different opinion of the maximum effectiveness of insulation. If money is no object and transportation is no problem, frame construction is very good indeed if done well. Be sure your roof will handle heavy snow loads. However, no frame cabin can ever have the warm feeling and classic, homey look of a log cabin.

For windows, the best construction I have seen is three panes of glass with dead air or a partial vacuum between. If you have only a single pane of glass in your ports, make up some sort of covering to place over them in winter. All my windows were single-pane thickness. I had a hinged shutter made of 3/4-inch plywood over one of my windows, with a stout bar that dropped in place to lock it. It would have kept out even determined intruders, and provided good insulation when in place. I had another of my three windows boarded up and the third, that I used the most, had the top covered with several layers of Visqueen with dead air, and the bottom was just a single Plexiglas panel so I could look out.

You will appreciate windows on all four sides of your cabin to be able to see what is going on outside without the necessity of leaving your cabin. While this probably seems obvious, I am surprised how many cabins one sees with two or even three walls with no windows at all in them. When you hear something big crunching around just outside your cabin it is wise to know what it is before you go rushing out to say hello. Alaska is the land of moose and bear. Bears don't usually knock, and moose are ready and able to kick you into next week if you let them. Put some sort of lookout on all sides of your dwelling, even if it's only a porthole. My old cabin had good windows on only two sides, and it seemed that when the moose came by it was always on the two sides that had no windows. I really missed a lot of the visual pleasure of winter on the lake because I could not see what was going on, on all four sides of my home.

At least two of your windows should be rigged to open, and ideally they should be on opposite walls of the cabin. This will give you a good breeze through the cabin on the warmer days of summer. It can get over 100 degrees in the Alaskan interior in midsummer. If you plan to be away from your cabin for any extended time it's a good idea to have stout wood shutters that close over the windows. These keep out prying eyes, extremely bad weather, and small critters. They won't stop a determined bear. If a big bear wants into your frame-constructed cabin he'll go through the wall. A log dwelling will slow him down a bit, but he'll still get in if he has time.

It's a good idea to have most of your window area on the side of the sun, which is to say the south side of the cabin. In fact, build your cabin on a south slope if at all possible. My old cabin sat on the north slope of a hill. A short distance away on the south slope of the hill the temperatures often got up to sixty degrees in early spring. It was twenty to thirty degrees colder at the cabin. Most summer mornings I had to build a fire to get warm. I took what I could find for my cabin at the time, but if I had been given a choice I would have chosen a cabin on a southern slope.

Ruthie and Andy Runyan had a moose try to come inside their cabin one day when the moose brought her new calf past the house. The cow moose may have been chasing one of their dogs, or just nervous at seeing the people there. Whatever the reason, she wanted in! The lesson is to be sure to provide yourself two doors to your cabin, one for the moose to come in, and the other for you to go out. Also, your main entry might get blocked with snow, said moose, or something worse!

Another good thing to try to incorporate into your cabin is a big overhang on the front porch. Cut your roof beams long, and extend the roof forward as you build it. About four feet should do it. An overhang is a real handy addition that costs very little to add to your home when you're building. The covered porch area is dandy for sitting under during a summer rainstorm or for watching the sun go down as the dew settles. It is also a handy place to hang your snowshoes or a quarter of a moose that you want to keep cool and out of the rain

. . . though you'll still need a proper cache. You can keep your saws and axes and a hundred other items under the overhang. I'm sure you won't regret having such a handy overhang on your front entrance.

Shortly after I arrived in Alaska I met an old-timer, a "sourdough" as they're usually called. I mentioned I was looking for a cabin. The first thing he said was, "Be sure to get near some good water." That was the best advice I got about cabins. Some day when you have nothing better to do, melt enough snow to make a cup of tea. You'll be surprised how much snow it takes. I've melted lots of snow trying to reduce the work of hauling water up a long, steep hill. Melting snow ain't no fun. And how will you get water in summer, pilgrim, if there's no open water near your cabin?

So, get your place situated on some water. Pick a big enough lake that it won't freeze solid to the bottom in winter, or a river large enough that it'll have some water flowing under the ice all winter. However, don't build so close to the water that you'll be flooded out come spring breakup. It is usually warmer some small distance above or away from any water, winter or summer. You must, of course, haul all your water uphill to your house, so choose your cabin's location and altitude with this in mind.

I spent my first winter hauling all my water up a sixty-foot hill by hand and I would not like to repeat the experience. I didn't have a snowmachine that winter and I didn't look forward to water day. The best thing about being on top of that hill was the fantastic view. I found that at my cabin the air was five to ten degrees warmer year-round than the air temperature at lake level. That, by the way, explains how it can be snowing heavily when it's 20 below. The air up high is ideal for snow generation, never mind what it's like where you are.

I think aesthetics are important in one's home, and doubly so in an Alaskan retreat cabin. Part of the problem with living in Alaska is putting up with the phenomenon known as cabin fever, which is a form of extreme depression caused by being confined in a small room for a long time. Every effort on your part to make your environment more pleasant will help reduce your depression. If you have to look at a wall for ten hours every day, would you rather look at a dirty, dusty, rough wood wall with your personal garbage draped here and there, or at a nice clean wall with some pictures and some of your own handicraft hanging on it? True, you don't really see the wall after a few hours or days, but the effects of it are working on you subliminally all the time. Why live in a grubby hole when, with a little thought and preparation, you can live in a pleasing environment? If you have a dumpy-looking home it'll play havoc with your nerves and sensitivities. Do a good job building and furnishing your cabin and it will pay dividends of satisfaction for many years.

If you have only a one-room cabin, the most efficient use of space is to leave the center of the room uncluttered. Array the tables, kitchen area, stove, bed, etc., against the walls out of the way. You'll do a lot of floor pacing, and if the center of the room is open you'll have a feeling of greater space than if it's cluttered with tables, chairs, etc. Many folks came into my little cabin and remarked that it was really big inside, after having said how small it looked from the outside. It was almost the Doctor Who effect, with his Tardis being bigger on the inside. It's something like living in a boat where space is limited and all of it must be used as efficiently as possible. Beds, for example, are stacked bunk-style, not spread out.

I needed only one bed, and that is all I had my first winter. My second winter I got smart. I got a bunk bed and I slept in the top bunk, up where the air was warm. The bottom bunk served as a couch and storage area for odds and ends. That helped solve the problem of my having no insulation in the floor.

Store your unneeded clothes and other items around the walls so they act as extra insulation. That first winter, without the bunk bed, the boxes of spare clothes that I had stashed under my bed went a long way toward providing me with a warm place to sleep. My extra junk was good insulation from the cold coming up through the floor. I had an old army spring cot with no mattress that first winter. I used an elk robe and two foam sleeping pads on the spring for a mattress and covered them with three army blankets. I then put my down sleeping bag on top of that, and made out okay. The second winter I got a real mattress to put on top of the springs and I moved my bed to the top of a bunk bed and it was a great improvement. If at all possible, get good commercial mattresses for yourself and for your family.

Ah, yes, the facilities. One often hears the question, "How do you go to the bathroom when it's forty below outside?" The obvious answer: very quickly. Procure for your outhouse a seat of Styrofoam. Nuf said.

One finds through experience that most problems with dealing with Alaska's cold are mental. If you let your mind run rampant it'll discover all sorts of things that'll keep you awake at night worrying. Heck, many folks who live in Kansas City or Toledo do that anyway! Problems about cold weather sort themselves out in time if you just put your mind to work overcoming them instead of making them bigger than they are.

In order to bathe, for instance, just get the cabin good and warm. Then strip down and take a "sponge bath" with basin and washcloth, just like we all did for many centuries, before we had running water in our homes.

I have mentioned the need to get your place near water. I lived on a large lake and, later, on a small river. My water systems were about the same in both locations. Once you have your water hole cut through the ice you can keep it from freezing solid overnight by covering it with a piece of plywood and then shoveling snow on top for insulation. Next time you want water you'll only have to bust a thin skin of ice. You won't have to recut the entire hole. I have already told how to make your ice hole in the chapter on tools.

For water storage inside the cabin, get a new plastic thirty-gallon garbage can with a lid. Label the can WATER. The label will keep most visitors from throwing garbage into your fresh water in well-meant gestures of tidiness. A drop or two of bleach will keep the water drinkable. Of course you can have as many water-storage containers for which you have room and ambition. But the water will get stale, so I prefer to keep only one water-storage can filled. I kept one area of the cabin for water storage and washing, and this kept the wet mess to a minimum. Note: the plastic garbage cans get very brittle in extreme cold. Thin plastic buckets and other tools are useless.

You'll have lots of time to read while living in your winter cabin. You'll get tired very quickly of poorly-written detective and western junk novels and will most likely relegate them to the fire where they'll do you more good. Select your reading material carefully, perhaps a bit deeper literature than you think you might like. Your time in the reading chair can be put to very good use. You'll enjoy top quality literature much more than escapist garbage, although this has its place when you need something to read that can get your mind off the weather.

Get a load of that chair! I found it at the dump, as I recall. It gave real comfort and also got my legs up off the floor. That's my good stove with an airtight iron door, flat top, and adjustable draft. A portable radio sits on the window ledge. It got station KCAM, Glennallen: that or nothing. A shortwave receiver would have been better. The book is one of the Destroyer series, not exactly the heaviest reading available, but great escapism.

A cheechako (greenhorn) once remarked how well-read were the people he talked with in the north country. Yes, we have a lot of time to read. I find myself reaching for the really thick books in preference to smaller ones. I have spent many long and happy hours huddled by the fire, poring over quaint and curious volumes of forgotten lore.

I suspect you'll find it's impossible to bring enough reading material north to Alaska. Many folks swap reading material cheerfully, but I prefer to buy my own books. I have encountered some very well-stocked libraries in tiny Alaskan cabins.

Heating Units

For about eight months of the year you'll have to provide twenty-four-hour heat for your Alaskan retreat. For the remaining four months you may want some early morning and late night heat source to take away the chill of those edges of the day. There are two main sources of heat in Alaska. One is wood and the other is fuel oil, or #1 diesel. On the average you can figure from three to five gallons a day will go up in smoke. There's very little chance in the foreseeable future that the price of heating fuel will come down, which makes it a good idea to plan on heating with wood at least part of the time if you are on any kind of budget at all (and who isn't?). This means you need two stoves, one for each kind of fuel. Let's first look at fuel-oil stoves.

My heating stove setup, wood and oil combined. This
is my second, and best, barrel stove. I welded a flat top
of 1/4-inch steel plate to it. The shared stovepipe gave
occasional trouble in lighting either stove if the other
was already going. Note the rack above the stove for
drying clothing. Also note the Visqueen on the walls
and on the false ceiling. There was no insulation in the
walls. The Visqueen kept out the wind but not the cold.
You can see my door-latch setup on the right.

OIL STOVES

I had the loan of an old military-surplus oil burner that measured about two feet square and stood three-and-a-half feet tall, and that old furnace worked very well indeed. It provided all the heat I ever needed in my little cabin, despite the lack of insulation. Most oil burners are quite simple and reliable. They consist of a burning chamber surrounded by a louvered housing that provides airflow past the hot burning chamber and, hence, airflow throughout the room. There is a carburetor to regulate the flow of fuel, with an adjustment to turn the flow, and hence the heat, up or down.

The carburetor is connected to the fuel supply, commonly a gravity-feed fifty-five-gallon tank located outside the cabin. This supply tank needs periodic refilling from some other larger source, either your own or from the place where you buy the stuff. Then there is the smokestack, which must be high enough to provide a good draft for the burner. The stack needs a counterweighted damper near the burner that opens or closes when the wind gusts past the stack. The damper prevents the fire in the chamber from being sucked out.

Such oil burners are very simple and foolproof. You'll want one to keep a minimum fire going in the cabin when you're away for a day or two and can't stoke a wood fire. It doesn't take much heat to keep things from freezing.

Check around when you get settled into your retreat cabin and you might find a good used oil burner. Your neighbor may have one he isn't using. He will also be able to give you tips on how to set it up properly, although there's no great trick to it. You can use a fifty-five-gallon drum for a feed supply, placed outside the cabin close to, and slightly above, the stove's location. Install a shutoff valve in the barrel at the outlet so you can turn off the flow when you want to. Many folks put a filter in the line at the barrel outlet, and that's not a bad idea. Be sure the oil filter is down-line from the valve so you can shut off the main supply when you want to clean or change the filter.

The height of the feed barrel should be arranged so its lowest point is about a foot above the carburetor. This "head" will provide positive feed to the carb at all times. Many carburetors have the recommended amount of head printed on them. Run a 3/8-inch soft copper tube from the tank twelve through the wall to the carburetor. This semi-flexible line provides an easy means of adjusting the position of the stove, and makes for a simple hookup. Don't kink the line or you might get a tight spot where water can collect and freeze.

You'll have to refill your supply barrel periodically from a supply tank that you've stashed somewhere handy, or from smaller drums of oil brought to your site, and the easiest way to do so is to use a twelve-volt electric pump driven from a car battery. A good electric pump is expensive but well worth it. I had access to one and found that in less than five minutes I could refill a fifty-five-gallon drum with it. That's about as long as I wanted to stand still last winter when it was 50 below. An alternate pump is the hand-powered lift pump, or wobble-pump, which requires lots of strong-arm effort on your part.

Instead of a fifty-five-gallon feed tank some folks set up their heating system with a 500 or 1,000 gallon feed, which requires filling only once a year. This sort of system requires water traps and filters to ensure its reliability.

If you have the usual fifty-five-gallon feed tank you can (and should) disconnect it completely once a year in the fall and dump all the water and dirt out of the tank that always get into it no matter how hard you try to keep it clean. Arrange the supply tank to have the stove-feed outlet slightly above the bottom, so any water that gets in the tank will settle below the tank's outlet. That way when it freezes it won't block the supply line. In warm weather you can simply dump it out.

Before you light your stove, every time you light it, check to make sure it's not flooded. This can happen if someone inadvertently turns on the carburetor's feed valve or temperature control valve and doesn't light the stove immediately. You must remove all the excess oil in the stove bottom before you light it. This is easily accomplished by removing the supply tube that runs from the carburetor to the burning chamber, usually at the rear of the burning chamber, and catching the oil as it drains out. Then reconnect the line, light the stove, and let it burn at low setting until the chamber and stovepipe get hot and start to draw properly. It is mighty disconcerting when a flooded chamber starts to go "Whoomp-whoomp!" as if it wants to explode, right after you light it. If this happens, turn off the supply at the carburetor, and let it burn out. If it is really bad you'll have to open the door of the chamber and let the surplus oil burn off while keeping your eye on the stack to see that it doesn't get too hot. This is extremely dangerous! Best not let this happen in the first place. There are no fire departments in the bush.

Periodically you should add a de-sooter, such as Meeco's Red Devil or Soot-Out to the oil. Follow the manufacturers' directions. Some of these chemicals are supposed to be added to the oil and some to the carb. It is a mess to have to clean a clogged stovepipe in any weather, let alone when it is very cold out, so don't neglect this simple maintenance item. In fairness I have to say I never cleaned my pipe on my oil stoves and I had no problems. Woodstoves are another story altogether!

Stovepipes only clog when it is the coldest it has been in six months, it's late at night, and you're fast asleep after the longest and most tiresome day you have had in three years. The only warning you'll get will be the burner flooding, or maybe the fire will go out when the soot falls down off the inside walls of the pipe and kills the fire. When this happens, you must take the smokestack completely apart, clean it and then put it back together. The blackest crud imaginable collects in the stovepipe. When you have to clean it, it will get on you, the rugs, the furniture, and the cat. This is not any fun. You will discover many new swear-words.

Perhaps the most common cause of fire in small cabins is the hot stack setting the adjacent wood on fire. Make sure your stack does not touch anything that can burn. One of the best ways to rig your chimney is to use commercial "Metalbestos" piping, which is a pipe within a pipe, with insulation between the two tubes. This pipe goes through wall or ceiling by passing through other metal bits and pieces that are well thought out, and also are adaptable to a great variety of setups. The only drawback is cost, but with such a setup you need have no worries about setting fire to your cabin. That's mighty cheap fire insurance.

I must say these Metalbestos setups are not the norm in Alaska. Most folks make do with some sort of jury rig which keeps the hot pipe away from the wood. The six-inch pipe on my stove ran straight up through a hole in the roof. The hole in the roof was large enough to clear the pipe by five inches all around. I used the bottom half of a fifty-five-gallon drum, inverted, to cover the hole in the roof, and the stovepipe passed through a six-inch hole in the bottom of the drum. The drum sat on the roof like a big steel hat with the stovepipe coming through it. It actually worked very well. It kept most of the water out, and also provided a long metal path between the hot pipe and the vulnerable wood roof. If I were building a cabin from scratch I would do the job right, however, and put in the best possible smokestack.

I had two stoves, one for oil and the other for wood. They shared the same smokestack, and somewhere in this book I have a photo of my setup. My first winter I used the oil stove only when I went to town for supplies. The second and third winters I used the oil stove much more because I was away from the cabin frequently, running a trapline. I had to buy fuel instead of scrounging wood, there being only so much time available to the busy trapper.

The woodstove did the bulk of the work of my two stoves that first winter. I had the two stacks joined inside, and ran only one pipe out through the roof. This worked well, but I suspect both stoves would have been more efficient without interference from the other. I sometimes had a hard time lighting the oil stove when the woodstove was going. It seemed like I couldn't get a good draft for the oil stove.

Oil burners come in all shapes and sizes and all seem to work well. I would get the smallest I could make do with, that took up the least space in the cabin. Some of the newer oil stoves are far more efficient than the old World War II surplus bruiser that I used. If you plan to rely on oil heat, get a big enough stove to permit its running on lower settings most of the time so it won't get too hot. If it is too small it'll run red hot all winter, which increases the danger of fire, and it still won't put out enough heat to keep you comfortable. It'll also create more carbon monoxide.

I once saw a fine old German stove with two chambers, one larger than the other. It was designed to provide two basic stoves within one unit: a big one for winter and a smaller one for summer or when just a little heat would do. Seems like a good idea.

WOODSTOVES

There are many kinds of woodstoves. Probably the simplest, and by far the most common, is the barrel stove. During the construction of the Alcan highway during WWII and in later years the building of the Alaska pipeline, the bush came to be dotted with used fifty-five-gallon barrels. These drums originally held every kind of transportable liquid, but usually oil or gasoline. These used drums dot the landscape even today in all corners of Alaska. They are the basis for the barrel stove.

To build a barrel stove you first acquire a good, stout barrel. Then you buy a kit that consists of cast iron door, stack outlet, and legs. Step three is to simply bolt the contents of the kit to your barrel, having poked the necessary holes. Barrels come in several thicknesses. Thick ones last longer.

I have seen some elaborate heating setups based on barrel stoves. Don MacArthur made a setup I admire. Don's stove has a steel plate welded on top to provide a hot pad for a coffeepot. It also has a built-in water heater, which consists of a copper tube inserted through the back of the stove directly into the fire area. This tube makes a loop or two inside the firebox and exits again out the back somewhat higher than the incoming tube. Both ends of the tube connect with a twenty-gallon water tank above the stove. The fire heats the entire twenty gallons by convection, and all one has to do is to keep the tank filled. As long as there is water in the pipe inside the stove the fire won't melt the copper tubing.

I also admire the Dawson family's stove setup, which consists of two barrels, one on top of the other, separated by a connecting stack about a foot long. The bottom barrel is the ordinary barrel stove, but the top one is filled with rocks. The smoke and hot air from the first barrel heat up the rocks, and then pass out through a conventional stack. The rocks hold and radiate heat that would have been lost up the stack, and they stay warm long after the fire has gone out in the stove below. It is a very comfortable cabin with a setup easy to duplicate. It would be a simple matter to install a door in the top barrel and use it for smoking fish and meats. The ideas are endless, and the barrel stove is one of the best heat sources available.

Put a layer of gravel in the bottom of your barrel stove and it won't burn through. Be sure your stove is far enough away from the wall so the stove can't start a fire in the wall when the stove runs red-hot. Keep the stove away from windows, which can crack from the heat. The same precautions on setting up your oil burner smokestack hold true for the woodstove. Stack maintenance is similar, but woodstoves create creosote in the stack.

Creosote is formed by burning wood with very little air. It forms inside your stove and in the stack. Creosote burns. If you let it build up inside your smokestack you'll eventually have a stack fire, which will get the stack extremely hot, and there is little you can do to put out such a fire once it starts. Be sure your stack is set up properly so it can't start your cabin on fire. Sparks on the roof are another common source of cabin fires.

It may seem I am harping about fire too much. This past winter some pretty impressive places burned to the ground near my home, including two lodges and a big warehouse, as well as several privately owned cabins. Fires start all too often back in the bush and there is little you can do to stop them once they start. Imagine this situation: you return half-frozen from running your trapline only to find your cabin fried to a fritter, nothing left but a blackened hole in the snow. It's fifty below and dropping, it's black as coal out, dawn is fourteen hours away, and your nearest neighbor is fifty miles away. What're ya gonna do now, pilgrim?

At the very least, keep some big extinguishers handy, keep them up to date, and be careful with fire!

Set up your woodstove smokestack with the corrugated parts of the pipe pointing down, so they fit inside the next lower stack piece. This will prevent the creosote from running down the outside of the pipe inside the cabin. Creosote smells foul when it gets hot, and if you make sure the creosote runs inside the next lower pipe you won't have that stink inside your dwelling. Put a screen on top of the pipe outside to keep sparks from setting your roof on fire. A conical rain hat at the top of your smokestack will keep most of the rain out of your pipe. Use guy wires to prevent the chimney from blowing away when the wind gets up.

I had a hard time getting a good fit of the door on my first barrel stove. It was a sheet-metal door, and it leaked air at the edges. The result was that the fire got too much draft. The wood burned too fast, though it got my uninsulated cabin very warm in no time at all. My next stove had a good cast-iron door. I went to a lot of trouble to seal it as well as I could and it had a nearly airtight fit, which was a great improvement. I also welded on a top plate of 1/4-inch steel after first cutting away part of the barrel. Finally, I gave the entire stove a coat of black stove paint. It looked great and worked as well as any commercial unit.

My old barrel stove would accept logs up to thirty inches long and eleven inches diameter. However, there are very few trees that size in the area of Alaska where I lived. Most of my trees were about five to six inches diameter, with a few up to about nine inches. I suspect most trees in interior Alaska are no larger than that. If you find bigger ones you can split them for faster burning or easier handling if you desire. I did exactly no log splitting. I was burning about a cord a week my first winter during a three-week cold spell, and I fed whatever I could find into the front of my barrel stove. That door saw some jumbo logs pass through it.

AIRTIGHT STOVES

Next, we have the so-called airtight stoves, some of which consist simply of a sheet-metal box with a door. They take up very little space, but they won't accept the big logs you can put into a barrel stove. These are sometimes called oilcan stoves, and they are fine for a tent camp or other temporary use, but useless for long-term home heating. These are little more than garbage cans with holes cut in them.

Some airtight stoves are rather expensive, but they seem to work quite well. They have useful flat surfaces, and also have fancy ducting, which provides more efficient heat transfer.

Probably the best of the woodstoves are the so-called Earth Stoves, which are big iron boxes with a clever air regulation system built in. This system regulates a damper that automatically increases or decreases the airflow to the fire as needed. The system incorporates a bimetallic strip, which requires no electricity. These keep a fire going for a long time and a very even flow of heat from the stove. They are quite expensive, but are very attractive and efficient.

No matter what kind of woodstove you install it'll take time to figure out how to run your system: how much wood to put in, how to set the air and stack dampers, what type of wood burns longest and hottest, and so on. There are a few rules to follow from the start, however.

When you're relying on wood for heat always have enough wood on hand for several days, and store it inside the cabin or, if outside, near the door. If you have this backup supply handy you won't have to worry about gathering wood if you get hurt, or if a severe cold snap hits and you don't want to go out. Late at night when the alcohol in the thermometer goes through the basement floor it's mighty comforting not to have to think about going outside for more wood.

Another rule: if you plan to be gone for a few days, always leave firewood and kindling ready inside, so you can get a fire going quickly and easily when you get back to the cabin. You never know what condition you'll be in when you return. You might not have enough strength to lift a piece of wood into the cabin when you get home. Plan for trouble before it happens. These ready fire makin's may someday save your life.

Incidentally, if you return to your cabin from a few days' jaunt and find someone sitting by your fire in your favorite chair reading your favorite book, don't be surprised. It's a rule of the north woods that you provide shelter for someone in dire need out in the bush, not by law so much as by common sense. It may be your turn next; you may get lost and stumble upon somebody's cabin when you most need it, and they're not home. You'll have no choice but to go in uninvited, maybe even break in. When you leave, be sure to leave your name and address and maybe some money for the food you used to help repay the unasked-for courtesy of the loan of the cabin. Be sure to replace any firewood you used. The guy sitting in your favorite chair was probably lost and cold, and needed a place to go for a while.

You'll usually have to get up in the night to add wood to your fire. It is a rare woodstove that will keep a fire burning for eight hours, and it is quite common for sourdoughs to spend many more than eight hours at a time in the sack during the long winter nights. You can figure on restocking the fire sometime during the night. Then when the cold again rouses you in the morning it's time to get up anyway, build a pot of coffee, and start the new day.

Many was the time I wished for a good wood cookstove. I was able to do a lot of cooking on top of my barrel stove and found it to be quite pleasant. I even baked bread in it. The only cookstoves I even heard of were too expensive, generally too big, and too far away. They can be a real pain, I am told, if you need a quick meal. I suppose they would be best used as auxiliary heaters, with a small fire going most of the time, then stoked with fresh wood when it's time to cook. I used a single-burner Coleman camp stove for most of my cooking, and I usually ate simple foods out of one or two pots and pans.

Probably the most convenient method of cooking in your retreat kitchen is with a propane stove, which usually has a built-in oven and three or four burners on top. You simply light the burners with a match when you want to cook.

One of the best ways to illuminate your cabin is with propane lamps, and because you are then dependent on a supply of propane you may as well cook with it. Propane lights are very efficient. However, if you run out of propane for any reason, you ought to have some alternate method of cooking figured out. An open fireplace is one possibility, but they don't do a good job of heating a cabin. It's possible to bake in a barrel stove, and I have pulled some amazing sourdough bread out of my old barrel stove. At least I was amazed! With some thought and planning and with the help of a welder, it's possible to install an oven into a barrel stove.

Some folks have experimented with coal heat, but with the lousy coal we get here in south-central Alaska such experiments didn't work out too well. The same amount of wood would have done as well, as one fellow found out to his costly dismay. He bought a big supply of coal and found that it didn't burn very well. Perhaps this situation will improve in the future. Better coal might become available, but I wouldn't count on it.

No matter what kind of heat unit you have, take apart the smokestack once a year, clean it, and replace any parts that may have rusted or become damaged. I used a BB gun to rap on my stovepipe to clean out the soot and creosote, but this dented the stovepipe and was not the best method. I was burning a lot of soft wood and I had a severe problem with soot buildup. In fact, one miserable night the stack became completely plugged and I had a nasty time finding the trouble and fixing it. I'll tell you all about it later, in the Journal portion of this book. Suffice to say you'll only have trouble when it's bitter cold, and at night.

Be sure you have good insulation in your cabin before you fire up your heating stove for the first time. It doesn't make a lot of sense to exhaust yourself all day gathering firewood and then huddle near the stove all night because the insulation is so poor you can't get the cabin warm. Been there; done that. You burn all your wood and get depressed from needless extra work. You sit by the fire with your legs freezing and your head burning, dreading the next wood-gathering excursion. It can be very enjoyable sitting by the fire when it's ungodly cold out, but not if you're constantly running out of firewood trying to keep up with the heat loss from poor insulation. Time and again you'll ask yourself, "What the hell am I doing here?"

Experiments with wind generators in south-central Alaska have met with poor success. There isn't enough wind on a regular basis, although when it blows it makes up for lost time.

Experiments with solar panels at Lake Louise, notably by the Runyan family, have been quite successful. Andy and Ruthie Runyan use solar panels to keep their radio batteries charged, run a TV, vacuum cleaner, microwave oven, copy machine, and lights. Occasionally they use a small generator in winter when they want to watch movies on the TV, and the batteries are down. But for the most part they are electric-energy self-sufficient.

Andy uses solar panels in his hunting camps on Kodiak Island and on the Alaska Peninsula to keep his two-way radio batteries charged. The Runyans are, in fact, in the process of obtaining as many twelve-volt home appliances as they can lay hands on. As the cost of solar panels comes down the panels will most likely be the best alternate energy source for future Alaskans. There is no lack of light in the Alaskan summers, and apparently enough even in winter to get good use out of solar panels.

Some day some diligent enterprising engineer will figure out how to provide heat and/or light from the vast potential provided by the temperature difference between outside and inside walls on each and every Alaskan cabin. When it is 50 below outside and 70 above inside, that's a 120 Fahrenheit-degree energy potential that ought to be able to be tapped. A giant thermistor of some sort built into the walls might be the plan. It's my bet the Japanese are working on this even now. At this writing they were making serious plans for a lunar base, and I suspect solar power and temperature-differential generators will play major roles on the moon.

Today there is talk in the science news of superconductivity becoming practical at near-arctic temperatures, with new alloys.

Formerly, superconductivity could only occur at temperatures near absolute zero (minus 459.4 degrees F.). At the very least, super-conductivity could provide low-cost transmission of electricity throughout the frozen north. This technology is possible today, but expensive.

To summarize: Get the best job of insulation possible in your cabin before you light that first match. Think about how to cook with wood and how to heat water with your heating stove. Get a decent oil heater and a good barrel stove or other wood-burning stove. Plan ahead for continued fuel supplies.

It's a mighty good feeling to sit in perfect comfort by your woodstove in the dead of winter, maybe reading a good book, with the knowledge that your heat has been provided by your own hands and cost you nothing but that effort. There's an undercurrent of excitement in the air when it's 40 below and growing colder. When you have a good supply of wood on hand and are perfectly happy, beholden to no one, the cold outside somehow adds to your feeling of security. It provides a counterpoint to your existence, an accent to your self-sufficiency. Experience it and believe.

Lights

$\mathbf{A}$s you sit in silent solitude in the far reaches of the north country, you will come to realize the necessity of something to read. In order to read, when one has only six hours of daylight at the most in the dead of winter, one must have some sort of artificial light. The best artificial light source other than electricity is propane. Propane lights burn silently and will provide all the light you are likely to need. To turn them on just strike a match, flip a lever to open the gas port, light the mantle, and you are in business. Each fixture is about the equivalent of a 100-watt bulb, and by locating several fixtures around your cabin you can have as much good light as any home anywhere in the world.

A propane system consists of a refillable tank located outside the cabin and as many individual lighting fixtures as you deem necessary inside. Copper tubing feeds each fixture. Two fixtures, one in the kitchen and the other in the main reading area, should give you about all the light you need.

Propane systems are efficient for day-to-day lighting and provide many hours of good light for your dollar. When supplies of propane are readily available, such a system is hard to beat.

You'll want an auxiliary light source both for portability and emergency use when or if you can't get propane. The Aladdin lamps run on kerosene or, with a slightly different mantle, on #1 diesel fuel, the same stuff you're burning in your oil stove. These are also quiet and efficient, and you can move them to wherever you want light.

Another lamp that uses diesel fuel is the old-fashioned wick-type lamp, and their only drawback is that they don't put out much light. Placing a reflector behind this type light makes them a lot more efficient, though, and they are a very pleasant and silent source of light. I have read several books by such light, though I would have liked more lumens. I have also read quite a bit by candlelight, though I can't recommend the experience. Candles ought to be in every home, for every good reason.

My lighting equipment, the kerosene lamp and the Coleman single-burner lamp that roared so loud. A metal-based kerosene lamp would have been safer than what I had. I also used candles on occasion.

Coleman gasoline lamps are next on our list to consider, and they put out lots of light. These burn what used to be called white gas, now sold as either Coleman fuel or Blazo (a Chevron product). Coleman fuel seems to work a trifle better than Blazo, but in much of the state Blazo is all you can get. Such fuels are very expensive in the bush, about $4 to $5 a gallon when I last bought some. The lanterns are fussy to light, and while they put out great light they burn with a most annoying roar that can drive you up the wall when you use these lights day after day. It's nice to be able to hear what is going on outside your cabin, and you just can't hear anything with the roar of a Coleman lamp in your ears. (You come to crave silence after only a short time in the bush. I spent three years at Lake Louise in near-absolute silence, and since then I have been unable to enjoy any sort of noisy music, much less dogs, noisy kids, etc.)

I have no experience with double-mantle Coleman lamps, but the single-mantle one I have has put out an abundance of light reliably for a good many years. In fact, all the Coleman products with which I have any experience have been top-quality.

With propane as your main light source and with some sort of auxiliary lighting that uses either kerosene or diesel fuel (or both), you will be pretty well set for cabin lights. You will, however, need some flashlights.

One of the handiest flashlights is the pocket-size throw-away kind (available throughout the north at the time of this writing) that come in an assortment of colors. They are shaped to throw their light at a 45 degree angle toward the ceiling while they rest on the table. They are small enough and useful enough that you should have one in your pocket whenever you leave the cabin. You can hold them in your teeth when you need both hands. I found them to be invaluable on the trapline. I also used a head-mounted light with a battery pack clipped to my belt, connected by a cord to the light. It was a nuisance because of the cord.

A really good high-intensity flashlight should be available in your cabin, and in the twenty-first century it must be one with an

LED bulb, or bulbs. One of the best is the mil-spec Fulton, or G.T. Price, angle-head, that takes two D cells. Buy a 30-lumen LED bulb from Amazon or wherever, drop it in, and you've got very reliable and handy lighting at your service. You can get adapters that hold AA batteries instead of the D cells in that same flashlight if you don't like the weight of the double Ds. There are other, far more powerful flashlights available that rely on rechargeable lithium-ion batteries that are more or less special-use items. They are fine if you have a way to charge 'em, but my recommendation is to stick to common batteries.

A small LED flashlight that takes AA batteries, or even just one, is a handy item, too. You'll use these a lot. In fact I'd never be without a pair of the AA-size flashlights, and though I used to keep a good supply of spare bulbs handy for them, the advent of LED bulbs makes that needless today.

Another type of flashlight to keep handy is the six-volt boxy flashlight that throws a beam as bright as daylight for a couple hundred yards, the kind that takes the big square six-volt battery with the springs on top. These put out a very strong beam, useful to see what is behind that pair of eyes over there on the edge of your night-time visibility. I have found the best of these to be the Star Railroad-Car Inspector's light. Be sure to drop in an LED bulb, and your batteries will last nearly forever. There are also now six-volt lead-acid rechargeable batteries that can be recharged with a small AC plug-in. Or just buy a bunch of common six-volt batteries. I use a 100-lumen bulb in my Star, but there are 40-lumen LEDs too that fit the six-volt torches that are far brighter than the standard incandescent bulbs of old. The 40-lumen bulb will extend battery life, too.

I have a penlight that rides in my shirt pocket wherever I go in the bush, and it is a well-used tool. I doubt that you can have too many flashlights.

Phil Cowan gave me a tip that I'll pass along to you. When you use one of the nearly universal AA-size pocket flashlights, such as the ubiquitous MagLite, you usually hold it in your mouth when you need both hands. Wrap the end of the flashlight body with a couple wraps of electrical tape to make a sort of pad for your teeth. Works great!

As I mentioned in the chapter on heating units, solar panels are the wave of the future. The Runyans have them and they love them. There is enough light in Alaska even in winter to get good use out of solar panels. I ran my computer and laser printer off their solar cell system and it worked to perfection. I had my old LaserJet II printer going, and it requires about 1,000 watts, and I had it on at the same time Mrs. Runyan had her microwave oven running. The solar panel system never even blinked. I hope to have solar panel lighting on any house I ever own, anywhere.

With solar panels becoming affordable, some folks are switching to rechargeable batteries for their flashlights. You can get rechargeable flashlight batteries in all sizes. If you're planning a solar panel setup, you might like to try rechargeable flashlight batteries. No matter what kind of flashlights you get, get several spare (LED) bulbs for each of them when you buy the flashlights. By the way, common alkaline batteries are also rechargeable now, with the right charger. Don't throw 'em away!

When it's very cold it's usually very clear. When the moon is full and the night is crystal clear, the intensity and beauty of starlight and moonlight on the snow are absolutely incredible. You have the clean air and the total silence and the complete stillness. It's 40 below and you like it. Once you've experienced this you'll never forget it.

Almost every night you can watch a display of the northern lights. Once in a very great while the dancing green curtain is so spectacular that it make you painfully aware of the existence of a force greater than any on earth, and you want to cry because the lights are so beautiful and they gently touch something inside you. One night I saw them like that.

The northern lights over Lake Louise. One can't help but want to return to the wilderness with the memory of such midwinter sights, like this, clear in one's mind.

Nothing is blacker than an overcast winter's night in bush Alaska. However, this condition very seldom occurs. Usually you can read and work outside in the moonlight with no auxiliary lights. However . . . I don't like to do much heavy reading outdoors when it's minus 40!

To recap: Check out the latest in solar panels before you buy anything. Other than free solar-powered electricity, the best general light for your cabin is propane, which is both efficient and quiet. Propane will also run your cookstove nicely. Next best is the Aladdin lamps, not as bright but quite good and also quiet. Coleman lamps come next, and though they are as bright as any other artificial light, their fuel is costly and the lamps are noisy. To one of the above sources of main light add a wick-type kerosene or diesel fuel lamp, making sure it's made with a metal base. Mine was glass and I feared it. Get some candles, and a good assortment of flashlights with LED bulbs. These should keep you out of the dark in the north country.

Food

You can't live off your rifles in Alaska. Alaska still has lots of game but it's spread out all over the place. You have to get to it before you can shoot it. If you're lucky and get a moose in the fall, you'll be well set for meat for yourself and your family during the coming winter. If you are luckier still and get a caribou along with the moose, you should have enough meat to eat for about a year. A moose may be too much for a single person, but you can perhaps trade for something else, or dry the meat for summer use. In the hunting area where I lived at Lake Louise, Game Management Unit 13, the caribou are doled out by permit. In the same area you can only take a moose if it is above a certain size. Cross the road and your moose has to be below a certain size. Regulations change from year to year, and sometimes change during the season itself. Get a copy of the current regulations each and every season to find out what and where you can hunt. Regulations are available from the Alaska Department of Fish & Game (ADF&G).

You might qualify as a "subsistence" hunter, and you are then permitted to take game that non-subsistence persons can't take. The subsistence issue is constantly changing, and may be nonexistent or strictly regulated in some areas. As of this writing subsistence hunting had been declared unconstitutional, but that might change. Make sure to check all game regulations with the ADF&G before you settle in for the winter to avoid confrontations with the game-law enforcement people, which is the Department of Public Safety/Division of Fish and Wildlife Protection (called "Protection officers"). In areas where there are no subsistence laws don't think you can bump off a moose or caribou whenever you want a change of diet. If there is no "dire emergency" at hand and you kill something not on the eligible game list you'll go directly to jail. The Protection officers are well-trained and tenacious, and they have a knack of showing up when you least expect them. It's poor business at best to attempt to cheat on your hunting. Cooperate with the Division of Fish and Wildlife Protection and you will discover them to be most helpful people. They'll go out of their way to help you if you are in need. You can get on one of their meat lists and can get some good meat in the form of road-killed moose or caribou.

There were some ducks on the menu if I got lucky.

If you are in dire need, which means that serious physical harm might come to you if you don't eat something right now, you can take game animals (or anything that happens along that you think might be edible) anytime and no one will complain. Be sure you really are in dire need. You are also entitled to defend yourself and your property against unwanted intrusion from wild animals, whether or not any season is open, or exists.

Here's an example of the Division of Fish and Wildlife Protection in action, which illustrates the uncanny knack of at least one of them being where he was least expected, to the surprise and consternation of an out-of-state poacher. I was camped with master guide Andy Runyan at his old cabin on Clarence Lake in the hilly country above the headwaters of the Susitna river. One morning I heard shots coming from the hillside above the cabin, so I set up the spotting scope to see what was going on. It was caribou season, and I was visiting with friend Runyan to rest and relax with him and a couple other friends. I got the twenty-power scope set up and, peering through the glass, clearly saw what was going on.

The shots I heard came from a group of out-of-state hunters as they fired into a herd of caribou. I watched one of their party shoot two caribou, then walk up to them and watch as they thrashed their last. He made no effort to put them out of their misery, just stood there watching them die. Then, to my utter amazement and considerable anger, he turned and walked away! He was leaving them to rot!

About that time Andy Runyan walked into camp from his morning hunt, took a look at the scene, and sympathized with my anger. If the guy had been in range I might have taken a shot at him, I was that upset.

Andy has a knack for accurate predictions. He predicted that our friend Mike M_____, an officer with the Division of Fish and Wildlife Protection, would be into camp that day and we could tell him our story. Sure enough, that afternoon Mike dropped in on us with his Super Cub. I told him my tale, and said I could pick out the guy from the clothes he wore, and that I was sure I could find the caribou. Mike said, "Let's go!" We got into his Cub and he flew us up toward the kill site to look things over. We spotted the dead animals from the air, and Mike was able to land the plane in a pothole lake near the scene of the caribou murders. We walked over to take a look.

Mike gutted them to save the meat and also tried to find a bullet, and I walked up the hill to see if I could find any cartridge cases where I had seen the man standing when he shot. I found three of his spent rifle cases and apologized to Mike, because I knew he had fired five shots. Mike was extremely happy and said we had a pretty good case against the fellow.

As luck would have it, about this time the party of out-of-staters came over the hill above us. As they approached I pointed out the murderer to Mike. Mike was in plain clothes. Mike did his incomparable number on the caribou murderer and got him to admit to what he had done, and I was extremely pleased to see the growing fear on the face of that jerk as he realized there had been a witness to his crime. It did my heart good to hear the quaver in his voice when he realized he was in the hands of the law.

Sad to say, the judge could only give him a fine and confiscate his rifle. If the judge had seen what I saw, the guy would still be in jail.

Fish and Wildlife Protection officers deserve our greatest respect and all our help if there is to remain any semblance of legal hunting in the state for future generations. The state is vast and the number of officers limited. Each officer has a very big job to do and lots of territory to cover. Help them and you are helping yourself. Their job is to ensure that there will always be plenty of game to hunt, and for our children to hunt as well.

You'll always find some anomalies in the regulation of game. For instance, you can shoot three black bear a year near Lake Louise, but you would be lucky to see even one. In three years trapping in the area I only once found black bear tracks. Why would I look for bear tracks in the snow? Sure, they den up in the winter, but sometimes they're out and about. One winter in January, VirgVial flew over a pair of grizzlies sunning themselves on a warm day. Andy Runyan shot a record grizzly off his trapline. He spotted the bear after it killed a moose in midwinter.

Duck season lingers months after the last duck has flown south. Rabbits are huntable year round, but are seldom seen in summer. Just because there is a season on something, don't think it's available. By the way, you can't shoot all the saber-toothed tigers you find. They aren't regulated and therefore are not legal to shoot!

Don't count on your hunting to feed you. This is not to say you have to support your local supermarket. You have a lot of options besides stocking up on canned or dried foods. Before I get into that, a few suggestions.

If you are setting up a "retreat," you should already know something about food stores. Freeze-dried foods ought to be well represented at your retreat, both for long- and short-term use. It is difficult to keep things fresh during the summer months in Alaska. You can't keep meat unless you dry, can, or smoke it. Canned or dried foods will keep indefinitely, and are probably the best bet for your summer meat.

The growing season is long due to the amount of sunlight, and the ardent gardener can raise some very nice veggies in a bush garden. You can also collect "wild" foods if you know what to look for. Fireweed is tasty at certain times of year. It tastes like spinach ought to taste. It's at its best in spring. In the fall, dried fireweed leaves make a dandy tea. Berries are available everywhere for the effort of gathering. Blueberries, cranberries, bearberries, currants, and rose hips all grow in abundance in Alaska. Most of the berries are best gathered after the first frost of the fall. Get a good book on wild foods and make a point of learning about these things and you will never regret it. There are some poisonous plants in Alaska, so get someone who knows to show you what is what, most especially concerning mushrooms, if you fancy them.

In addition to your freeze-dried foods and free wild plant gatherings, you ought to lay in a good supply of canned goods. Some of the supply centers in the north are geared toward quantity buying, and they will give good prices on case lots of your favorite canned goods. Most stores throughout the state sell such items as pickles, peanut butter, mayonnaise, and syrup in gallon jars or cans, and this is the cheapest way to buy such things. You need to get away from the notion of making a quick trip to the corner grocery each day, as so many city-dwellers do.

Beans, rice, oats, split peas, flour, and cornmeal are a few of the dry foods that should be in your larder in large quantities. Dried onions, potatoes, and milk are a few others. I have lived on rice and tomatoes with maybe an onion and some bacon grease for very long periods of time with nothing to supplement this. I can't recommend this as a good diet, but I hasten to add I am never without a good supply of both rice and beans in the cupboard. Such things are cheap and should be obtained in large quantities and stored so the mice can't get at them. Large glass jars work well.

The traditional way to store your food is in a properly built cache, the little log cabin on stilts near the main cabin that we see in so many paintings of wilderness cabins. They keep the bears out, and if you have some aluminum flashing or old stovepipe around the legs, then the squirrels and other critters can't get up the legs. You reach your food stores with a ladder.

In some areas, ambition permitting, you can dig an underground cellar, but first ask your neighbors if this is feasible. In some places, if you cut through the permafrost you'll sink into a bottomless bog. You might find your entire cabin slowly sinking into the hole you so carefully dug. When the ground condition makes such a hole practical, it will provide a cool spot much like a refrigerator year-round, the temperature staying around 40 degrees.

One of the best food sources in Alaska is fish. The bigger lakes have lake trout, Dolly Varden, lingcod (burbot), whitefish, and in some areas, northern pike. In summer, all the streams have grayling, rainbow trout, and of course, salmon. If you are near any decent water, which of course you should be anyway, there is no excuse for going hungry in Alaska.

At Lake Louise, the fishing goes something like this: in fall you set out a net for whitefish. These will provide not only good eating, but also bait for bigger fish. Once you have laid in a good supply of whitefish and have frozen them, you can pull your whitefish net and forget it until next year. Natives like raw whitefish and eat them frozen, like scaly ice cream bars. They can have my share.

Ice fishing is very productive. To catch a fish through the ice, you use a chunk of the frozen whitefish for bait, the fresher the better, fishing on the bottom for burbot or slightly off the bottom on a tended line for lake trout. Burbot fishing is the easier, for you can leave the line or lines (up to fifteen, though this is usually wasteful) overnight with a reasonable expectancy of a fish by morning. If you expect to get a lake trout you should be ready to set the hook for best results. Again, check fishing regulations with the Alaska Department of Fish & Game. As this is written, the burbot fishing in Lake Louise is prohibited because of over-fishing.

My first fish, a lingcod (freshwater burbot). I had not yet built the front porch for the cabin.

Though an odd-looking fish, the burbot is fine eating. Some prefer lake trout, and these are occasionally caught on a burbot set. A better way to get lake trout is to troll for them in summer, using big spoons or the famous Alaska lure, which is a big chromed plug. There are a few lakes where it is possible to catch lake trout on flies, and I have done so and have photos to prove it, but spin fishing with spoons is usually your best bet.

Almost every stream in Alaska contains grayling, that pleasant-looking trout-family member with the big dorsal fin. When I was employed one summer as a fishing guide on the Gulkana River we found an abundance of hungry grayling all along that river. We had quite a time finding a lure they would not take. They would hook themselves on everything from the tiniest dry fly to some six-inch spoons. My partner, Ed Eggleston, could not believe that the little grayling would hit that big spoon, which was a third as long as the fish. Ed hooked quite a few grayling on it when he was casting for salmon. I won a bet with one of our clients that I could hook a grayling with one cast of my fly rod, using a dry fly.

Most Alaskan streams contain some grayling, and fly-fishing is the best way to hunt them. They usually rise in the late afternoon and a mosquito or black-fly pattern laid gently on the water just above their most active rise area will net you a grayling in short order. I personally prefer the fly rod for rainbow as well, and I had good luck with a wet fly Andy Runyan gave me that resembles two salmon eggs. Mickey Finns also work well on rainbow.

The salmon runs occur throughout the summer, the reds and kings being the first up the river. A little later the silver, or coho, salmon make their run. Any of these ocean fish will give you your money's worth with hook and line, but I think the red, or sockeye, salmon to be the best fighters, pound for pound. An eight-pound red will fight like a twenty-five-pound king. The closer to the ocean you catch these fish the better the fight you will have on your hands.

If you don't have a boat you can do okay fishing from shore. You simply must have your line in the water to catch fish. This may sound like the most glaringly obvious statement in this book, but bear with me a minute. On one of my trips guiding fishermen down the Gulkana I had a client who just couldn't understand why he wasn't catching fish. His buddies caught everything the river had to offer, but this guy felt left out. He was the most tentative fisherman I've ever seen. Every so often he would fling his line into likely spots, then reel in to find nothing. He would then sit and sulk for an hour or two, and then try again. I guess he wanted the fish to jump into the boat.

Nothing beats consistent effort in fishing, or in any other enterprise known to man, for that matter. Keep on casting, keep your line in the water, and you will catch fish.

I have caught lake trout fishing Lake Louise from shore. In fact I have caught more lakers when I was fishing from shore than I have by trolling, though none of the shore-caught fish were really big. The big 'uns keep to deeper water, and you must fish deep with big lures if you would catch them.

When I fish Alaskan rivers for salmon I have the best luck using big artificial lures, big spinners and spoons fished into the deep pools of the rivers. Some folks like salmon eggs for this fishing, but I haven't had anywhere near the luck with eggs that I have had with spoons. I let the lure go as deep as I can. King and red salmon like to lie near or on the bottom of these pools. You may have to drag your lure across their noses quite a few times, especially with tired red salmon, to get them interested enough to take a bite. Be patient. When they hit, you'll know it.

You must use big tackle to catch Alaska's big salmon, although you can have a grand time with light gear if you really don't need the fish. I watched Al G___ fight a king with lightweight tackle for over an hour by the clock. Finally the king decided he'd had enough. Down the river he went, cutting the line on a sharp rock to make his escape. Al had one helluva fish story to take home!

As you come to grips with the weather of the north country and spend a good deal of time out-of-doors, you come to crave some sort of edible fats. You can lay in a supply of canned margarine, butter—or coconut oil if you have the money—and you can also save your bacon grease, which is very good and easily digested. Another edible fat is obtainable from grizzlies or black bear, and I am told either of these is very fine cooking fat indeed, although I have no personal experience with either. Seal oil is another possibility, though at present seals are protected.

Bring with you good supplies of salt and pepper, plus your favorite spices, as all these are hard to get when you are back of beyond.

Two other items bear mention, neither of them strictly food. One is vitamins. I find that I feel a whole lot better when I am taking a multivitamin regularly. There are some vitamins and minerals lacking in the commonly available food up here, and when you add to that the lack of sunlight, you'll find you need a dietary supplement of some kind.

The other item is alcoholic beverages. The cost of booze in the bush is prohibitive. Some areas are "dry," with no alcoholic beverages sold at all. If you must have your sundowner, you can expect to pay a premium, up to ten times what you could get it for in supply centers such as Anchorage. Anyone who has spent ten or twelve hours in one day on a trapline when it's 50 below will be more tolerant of drink and drinkers, and can understand the significance of a good stiff one before dinner. Alaska already has an overabundance of alcoholics, and I am not recommending that anybody join their ranks. Used intelligently with moderation, good whiskey or brandy has its place in the far north. Just be sure to never drink before you go out into the cold. Do so only when you're safely at home again.

While it is possible to get by with just a frying pan and a pot, you will do a better job of preparing your meals with a nested set of pots capable of holding a good quantity of stew or whatever, with other pots for vegetables and so on. I brought a set of aluminum pots and pans up the Alcan with me in a homemade canvas bag, and I have been well-served and well satisfied with them. These don't need to be expensive and certainly not fancy, just durable and preferably unbreakable.

In addition to your pottage, you need a good coffeepot. Not Mr. Coffee, please. It's common courtesy to invite any passers-by in for a cup, and your coffeepot will get a lot of use. Remember that it will spend much of its life sitting on the back of your stove, so get a good metal coffeepot. You also will need plates, and while ordinary porcelain or china plates are nice, the cheap aluminum ones that come with a nested pot set won't break when dropped. I was given a set of fine unbreakable porcelain dishes by Ken and Phyllis Weyand some time back, and I'm still amazed by 'em. I accidentally dropped one of the bowls on my kitchen floor and watched it bounce and ring all over the kitchen. It didn't break, and I still don't believe it. So it isn't absolutely necessary to eat off of iron dishes.

Nothing I have ever found in an unbreakable coffee cup compares with a decent porcelain or pottery cup. I have tried enameled tin cups, Sierra Club cups, plastic cups, Styrofoam cups, and on and on. I insist on a decent, civilized coffee cup. Incidentally, the best use I have found for those shallow stainless Sierra Club cups would probably get me strung up at one of their meetings: I use it to scrape crusted snow off the top of my traps on the trapline!

Some of the propane cooking stoves have a built-in oven, and these stoves are probably the best way to do your cooking. There are three or four burners on top that you light with a match. Such a stove is a convenient and efficient way to cook. Watch out for leaks in your setup, and be sure not to have your tanks overfilled. This can lead to leaks, explosions, and fires that can cost you all you possess . . . even your life if you get caught.

A careful selection of stored foods, some emergency dried foods, and a little hunter's luck in the fall together with your fishing efforts ought to keep you well-fed year-round.

Guns

GUNS FOR THE LAST PIONEERS

(Reprinted from the February 1980 *The American Rifleman*)

The barrel stove sends last night's damp chill flying from my wilderness cabin. A fresh pot of coffee adds its warm smell to the room, while outside the wind plays a tune on my stovepipe. It is mid-spring as this is written, and I'm still suffering the doldrums of post-winter letdown, trying to get used to the fact it's no longer 70 degrees below zero outside, as it was a few short weeks ago. But the cold was part of the price I chose to pay to be able to enjoy firsthand some of the finest hunting left on earth. This is wild country. This is Alaska.

While it isn't necessary to live through an Alaskan winter to be close to the hunting, many people are planning to come and live up here to get away from the meaninglessness of humdrum lives at least temporarily and to personally experience one of the last frontiers. These modern pioneers will surely bring with them a vast assortment of firearms with which to pursue Alaska's big game: some good and some not so good. Today's pioneer has a much wider choice of weaponry than did the early settlers, who were well instructed to get a Hawken rifle as their prime hunting tool. In addition to hunting big game, today's settler or adventurer will probably want to be equipped for small-game hunting, water-fowling, and pest control. Many of the new settlers will be seeking advice on what guns to bring up, or what new guns to buy to best cover all Alaskan hunting situations. Is my 30-06 adequate, or should I get something bigger? Do I need a 458 Win. Mag.? What shotgun? And what about sidearms?

My qualifications to advise on such a potentially controversial subject consist of more than ten years' serious contemplation of a move to Alaska, together with a lifetime of firearms study and discussions with Alaskan residents, hunters, and vastly experienced Alaskan big-game guides. In addition, I have studied the writings of intelligent hunters of great experience in Alaska, the states, and Africa for more years than I care to mention and I have compared their findings with my experiences. Here, then, are my recommendations for an Alaskan battery for the modern pioneer.

First, to select the big-game rifle, consider the game. Alaskan moose are the biggest "deer" in the world, running well over half a ton weight. Caribou are the size of a big mule deer or small elk. The Dall sheep are not huge but are certainly hardy, as is anything that can live through an Alaskan winter. Then there are the bears, the largest on earth. Some argue that a small rifle will kill everything, but I believe the biggest rifle one can shoot well is the best choice because it will probably kill all sizes of game more swiftly and hence more humanely. I consider the 338 Winchester Magnum in a good bolt-action scoped rifle to be the best tool for general Alaskan big-game hunting. Factory ammo, well distributed throughout the state, is available in 200-, 250-, and maybe 300-grain weights at 3,000, 2,700, and 2,400 fps respectively. In addition, the handloader can add the intermediate weights of bullets, as well as several weights of the excellent Nosler Partition and, today, quite a few more excellent bullets, easily found for the 338 caliber rifles. He will have an easy time finding components throughout most of the state. I believe the 338 Mag. will perform adequately on Dall sheep, caribou, moose, goat, and both black and grizzly bear, assuming proper bullets and good shooting.

I love single-shot rifles and, of course, double rifles, but I feel the bolt-action is a more versatile gun for all-around use with scope. I feel the bolt rifle requires good positive extraction for repeat shots should the need arise. I have had modern extractors fail me twice, and that is two times too many. On dangerous game it could have been fatal to have the extractor fail to extract a spent case. For this reason I favor the controlled-feed Mauser-style full-length extractor on all my big-game bolt action rifles.

I recommend that the one-rifle hunter buy at least a spare striker and extractor when he buys his rifle, and that he take time to learn how to install them. Distances are long and mail delivery is sporadic in interior Alaska. While there are many gun shops located throughout the state, you may not be able to get to them when you most need to. In fact, the wise man would also procure the most-likely-to-break parts for all his guns and take them along, just in case.

I strongly recommend that all scope-sighted hunting rifles be fitted with auxiliary iron sights, and I have all my scoped rifles set up that way. Backup sights are doubly important for any Alaskan hunting rifle. I well remember loaning my old 338 to Ken D____ just after I had come back from a Montana sheep hunt. Ken was going after big Colorado elk and had no suitable rifle, so I let him take mine. Ken got a chance for a shot at an elk, raised the rifle, and could see nothing. Ken was in a driving snowstorm at the time, and he thought it was snow on the scope. He swabbed off the scope on both ends to no avail. He couldn't see through the scope because it was internally fogged. I had dropped the rifle and damaged the scope on my hunt in Montana, though I didn't know it. The scope gave me no problems in Montana, but it fogged up completely when Ken took it up into the Colorado mountains. Although Ken did not get that shot, he removed the scope and continued hunting with my rifle, using its iron sights. It seems when something goes wrong with your equipment it always does so at the worst possible moment and location.

There are portions of coastal Alaska where heavy snowfall is the rule, not the exception. It may be a good idea to consider detachable or swing-away mounts for your scope if you plan to settle or hunt where it snows much of the time. There may be times when you'll find it more convenient to hunt with iron sights than to be constantly cleaning off snow. I have quick-detachable mounts on most of my rifles, and I like them. I have used the Jaeger single-lever mount, Griffin & Howe side mount, the old Leupold Detacho mount, and the Pilkington device, to name a few. There are a few more good ones out there.

Two other popular calibers in Alaska are the 7mm Remington Mag. and the 30-06. Ammo for both is well distributed in Alaska. If I had to choose between these, I'd take the 30-06 for two reasons: better ammo distribution, and heavier bullets available. I can hear the critics already howling that the 7mm has more "energy" than the '06 and is therefore "more rifle." I confess to having very little faith in paper ballistics and prefer to put that faith in good bullets of good weight at reasonable velocity. It is the bullet, after all, that does the work on the game, not the powder bottle that holds it in the rifle. While some may think the 30-06 or 7mm Mag. is enough rifle for all Alaskan hunting and will kill anything one might encounter, there might come a time, as even the late small-bore advocate Jack O'Connor said, when a man wants to stop a grizzly faster than he can with either of these two cartridges.

The only reason for not choosing the 338 Mag. over anything smaller is fear of recoil. While it is true that heavier bullets produce more recoil energy than light ones, all else being equal, it is also true that most fear of recoil is mental. Many times I have had friends shoot one of my heavy rifles, 375 on up, and they'd tell me the big rifle had nowhere near the recoil they anticipated. The usual comment is, "Hey, that's not too bad! Gimme another round."

Don't be afraid of the recoil of a 338 rifle, or even the 375 H&H. Pay no attention to the comments some guy behind the counter or at the rifle range might throw your way about big rifles crunching bones and all that nonsense. Once in Montana I was checking the sighting of my 338, one of the light post-'64 M70 Winchesters, alongside a friend who was shooting his light Remington M700 30-06 with no recoil pad. We swapped rifles for a few shots. We discovered his light '06 was far less comfortable to both of us than was my 338. The same guy recently shot my rather light (8-1/4 pound) 458 Win. Mag. He said, "What have I been afraid of all these years!"

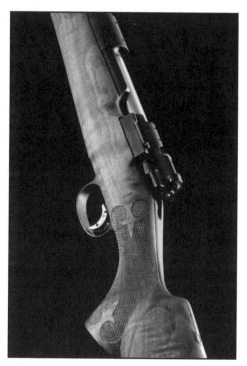

This is my favorite bolt-action rifle, caliber 338 OKH (a wildcat) on a Mauser 98 action. Note the extended tang on top. Instead of a wildcat like this I recommend the 338 Winchester Magnum because it's a standard cartridge with ammo easily available. Such a rifle is probably adequate for all Alaska's big game. Nothing smaller will suffice. That's my woodwork and checkering.

The only other cartridge I would consider besides the 338 Mag for an all-around Alaskan hunting rifle is the 375 H&H Mag. The 375 will probably cost more, because these cartridges require a longer action, which is generally more expensive, and all makers generally charge a premium for building a 375. Ammo is very well distributed and easily available throughout Alaska for the 375, and anyone possessing a good bolt-action 375 H&H Mag has as fine a rifle as any for all-around Alaskan use.

The 416 Remington Mag has become popular in Alaska, and if you can take its recoil you won't go far wrong with one of those. However, the 338 Win Mag or 340 Weatherby will probably have a flatter trajectory. They also, depending on the bullet choice, can have better retained energy at long range than the 375. With bullet selection so good in 416 caliber after the introduction of the 416 Remington round, one might consider the wildcat 416 Taylor (on a shorter action) weighing about eight to eight-and-a-half pounds, scope and all. That cartridge is basically the 458 case necked down to take 416 bullets. Note that any cartridge you choose can be loaded down to give added versatility. I carried a light 458 Winchester Mag stoked with 350-grain bullets during my later years in the Alaskan bush and it served me very well.

In addition to the centerfire big-game rifle, one will find plenty of uses for a good accurate 22 Long Rifle repeater. The 22 will not only put such excellent food as ptarmigan and rabbits on your table, it can also double as a varmint rifle within reasonable range. Many outback dwellers like to raise a garden, and the 22 will effectively keep "varmints" out of the vegetable patch, especially when you use the high-speed 22's such as Stingers. I have found 22 ammo to be excellent trading stock even today in Alaska. I have used a few boxes of 22 ammo to buy the labor of a stout youth; I was happy for the help, and he was happy to have something to shoot. A good 4X scope will be a benefit on the 22 rifle.

Me on webs (snowshoes) going after small game with my 22 LR custom Winchester M69A rimfire rifle. This rifle fed me many times.

The only other rifles a prospective newcomer to Alaska might want to consider are specialized ones for limited use, such as a long-range, heavy-barrel rifle capable of killing varmints and fur bearers up to the size of a wolf at extreme range; or a very heavy-caliber rifle if you expect to settle in bear country, or make a practice of hunting them. For the long-range rifle I suggest a heavy-barrel 220 Swift, fitted with 3X-9X scope, or 6X fixed power.

For bear country, the biggest rifle ever made may be none too big under some conditions. You must, by state law, have a guide with you when hunting grizzly your first year in Alaska. From then on, you're on your own. It doesn't take much asking around before you find out how hard it is to stop a determined bear, and how miserably some seemingly heavy (read: high muzzle energy, sounds-good-on-paper ballistics) rifles actually perform under emergency conditions. My friend Andy Runyan, a Kodiak bear guide of great experience (a Master Guide), tells his clients to bring whatever rifle they can shoot with confidence to accurately place their bullets on the great bear, because Andy is there with his backup rifle to prevent things from going wrong. His backup rifle is a 404 Barnes-Johnson Express, a wildcat that throws a 300-grain bullet at over 2,800 fps. It is a lot of rifle, and Andy is fond of it. But as soon as he laid eyes on my 470 double rifle he tried to talk me out of it to use as his bear gun. The wise old bear hunters will always use the biggest rifles they can get their hands on, and they're not afraid of their rifles. One old-timer told me with pride that his 450 Alaskan would shoot through any bear. Another guide made up a big .40-caliber wildcat after a smaller rifle nearly got him killed. And so it goes. Those with experience on the big bear use big rifles.

Next, consider the handgun. I firmly believe in carrying a heavy sixgun at all times when out in the Alaskan bush. By heavy sixgun I mean 41 Mag, 44 Mag, or heavy-loaded 45 Colt such as the Linebaugh Conversion. I don't consider any other handgun cartridges even remotely useful for potential use against a bear, especially the 357 Mag and 45 ACP—though the 45 ACP is useful in town for two-legged varmints. However, since this was first written I bought a 500 Linebaugh, which was both handy and extremely powerful, as is the 475 Linebaugh. Recoil of those two is not for the faint of heart. Built on the Ruger Bisley frame, they are not over-big like some of the huge and heavy handguns available from major makers. They are thus more likely to be carried. John Linebaugh well knows his business, as does Hamilton Bowen, who also makes handy handguns for John's cartridges.

There are still those who think you can't hit anything with a handgun. I suggest they attend a handgun metallic silhouette match to discover the error of their ways. But even many knowledgeable handgunners think it's foolish to carry a handgun for protection against a bear attack because you might be tempted to actually shoot the bear. True, if you needlessly wound a curious bear you will be in serious trouble, with either the unhappy bear or the Alaska Division of Fish and Wildlife Protection, in neither case a happy position. Because I have taken the necessary steps to train myself to shoot a heavy sixgun fast and accurately (years of competition with full loads in 44 Mag sixguns, many thousands of rounds both from rest and drawing from holsters as fast as possible, including double action aerial work on hand-thrown targets, and also IPSC competition, when it used to mean something), I feel I stand a pretty good chance of surviving a determined and unexpected bear attack from close quarters if I am armed with a good sixgun. Unarmed, I would have no chance at all. Accordingly, I pack a sixgun all the time. If I go on a planned bear hunt I'll take a big rifle, but I'll still have the sixgun on my hip.

Another reason for packing a powerful handgun is for the personal confidence it will give the man practiced in its use. Animals seem to have an uncanny ability to read your mind, which I've noticed countless times. If a bear sees you and senses that you're not just another harmless creature, I think he'll be more likely to leave you alone than if he senses that you are in mortal terror of him.

During the winter when the bears are asleep (at least most of the time), and you wish to be out hunting small game, exploring, or trapping, you might find use for a 22 pistol. Anyone wanting a 22 LR pistol today has a very large and perhaps confusing selection from which to choose, same as with the 22 rifle. If you need a hint or two, I would look hard at the all-stainless Kitgun by Smith & Wesson, and also at Bill Ruger's Standard auto, one of the finest and most reliable of all 22 auto pistols. My personal all-time favorite 22 handgun is the Smith & Wesson K-22 revolver with the six-inch barrel. However, the handloader can produce light loads for the heavy handgun and thus make do with only one handgun.

Next we come to the shotgun. Any sportsman coming to Alaska will want a shotgun. In Alaska we have some very fine duck and goose hunting, as well as fine grouse, ptarmigan, and snowshoe rabbit hunting. Seasons are long and limits large, and the avid wingshot will find many opportunities to engage in his sport. My personal choice is a 12-gauge double, bored modified and full. I like the handling qualities of a good double over all other types of gun.

If the choice is a pump or auto, I would likely choose modified choke as the best compromise. Better wingshots than I would undoubtedly recommend more choke, and poorer shots would want less choke. I have found that with full-choke guns I can always wait out the bird, given relatively open country. While some of Alaskan wingshooting is in heavy timber, more of it is over open water where the full-choke guns and good shots have their day. If one were concentrating on pass-shooting waterfowl on the salt flats on the coast, more choke rather than less would be the order of the day. But for walked-up ducks and inland game such as grouse and rabbits in the woods, one would be better served with improved cylinder choke or, at most, modified in a one-barreled gun. You might consider having one of the variable choke devices installed for increased versatility with the single-barrel gun. It's easy to see the advantages of the double gun as an all-around shotgun.

For versatility and availability of ammo, in Alaska as elsewhere, it's hard to beat the 12-bore. For those who need a lighter gun, the only choice is the 20 gauge. Again I base my choices on ammo availability throughout the state.

If you plan to live near Anchorage you may be able to get ammo for numerous odd gauges and rifle calibers that I haven't mentioned. If you reload, and I suggest that you should, you can make do with many odd calibers or wildcats; but one day you just may run out of components or ammo when far from your loading bench as I did once, hunting antelope in Montana. I had a 264 Win. Mag, not the most popular caliber, and I mistakenly shot up all my hunting handloads while doing some long-range testing on the Montana prairie. I was lucky to find some factory ammo in a small country store, and I was able to continue hunting with that flat-shooting rifle.

There is a tendency, when one speaks of a firearms battery of any sort, to want to list a different gun for each game animal and condition encountered. I have tried to avoid that, and in so doing it may seem I have tried to idealize a few firearms. I realize there is no such thing as an all-around gun, and I hope my suggestions will not be taken as such a recommendation. If you have your own special shooting sport you'll know better than anyone else what you need in the way of equipment. But for the sportsman contemplating settling in Alaska and wanting to equip himself fairly well to enjoy Alaska's varied hunting, the firearms suggested here will prove themselves equal to any task to which one might set them.

(End of *The American Rifleman* article.)

To reiterate, get a good bolt-action 338 Winchester Magnum centerfire rifle with detachable scope and iron sights. If you don't mind extra weight and cost you might consider a 375 H&H Magnum, and if you can take the recoil, maybe one of the 416 calibers. Get a 22 LR repeating rifle that is reliable and accurate, and be sure it has both iron sights and provision for a scope. Get a good 12-gauge shotgun; a double gives you the best instant choice of choke. Get a big sixgun and wear it always, and I suggest 44 Magnum caliber or larger. Make your choices of guns rugged and reliable, test them before you go to Alaska, and get spares for everything. Good luck and good hunting.

DEFENSIVE GUNS

Some years ago I wrote some paragraphs about what you might need in the way of guns for the possibility of a declining civil order. At the time the biggest threat seemed to be the Soviet Union. Today it well might be our own government, if things keep going as they are. At any rate, there are some specific guns you might want to consider that I didn't mention in my Alaska-guns article.

I wholeheartedly recommend you obtain and read a copy of Mel Tappan's excellent book *Survival Guns* (The Janus Press, PO Box 75455, Los Angeles, CA 90075; Library of Congress Catalog Card No. 75-17327), for a more extensive discussion of all types of firearms suitable for your retreat. Tappan discusses many specific guns, why you may need them, and what modifications you might want to consider to make yourself as ready as possible for any sort of civil disorder.

Remember this: The more remote you are the less chance there will be for anyone to come a-knocking uninvited. If you expect social disorder or anything approaching it, get your retreat as remote as you can. It could be argued that if you are sufficiently remote there is no need for battle rifles and other military-style firearms. Bear in mind that there are thousands of small private airplanes in Alaska that could be used to reconnoiter backcountry dwellings to pinpoint likely strike zones for follow-up land attacks by organized groups of looters. You could also be attacked by just plain bums at any time of year, social disorder or no.

In the event of widespread problems of serious significance it's a very likely prospect you'll have to defend what you have, no matter where on earth you may find yourself. In short, *Be Prepared.* This means get a good combat rifle and enough ammo (1,000 rounds is the usual recommendation) and stash them at your retreat. Get some spare magazines and keep them loaded. Provide yourself with spare parts when you buy the rifle and take the time to learn all you can about your combat guns, including how to repair them in the dark. I'm perhaps not qualified to comment on family matters because I don't have a family. However, it seems like a good idea to provide serious guns for every member of your family who is capable of handling one.

For serious use I can only suggest the 308 (7.62 mm NATO) caliber in available semiautomatic rifles. Leave the 223 (5.56 mm) for the kids and the ladies if they can't handle anything bigger. If you must have a 223 rifle, why not make it a varmint bolt-action and get some good use out of it. Get something like a Ruger Mini-14 for a spare rifle if you like, but not for use as a front-line defense rifle.

In times of prolonged lack of resupply, you may find that the only ammo you have left is military stuff, and for this reason it is prudent to have a good accurate sporting rifle with scope that will accept your 308 ammo.

I would also provide myself with at least one good 45 automatic with at least six magazines and a good supply of ammo for same. With more than sixty years of testing guns behind me, I have personally found the 1911-style 45 auto to be the finest fighting handgun in existence. I've trained and competed with it, qualified for the Colorado IPSC team with it, and have put a great many thousands of rounds through a variety of 'em. (Although some consider a good revolver to be superior in reliability to any auto-loader, I've had revolvers lock up.) I consider the Colt Government model 45 automatic (the 1911 and its clones) to be the finest of all automatic pistols. Some of the shorter and lighter versions like the Lightweight Commander or copies thereof are easier to pack all day, and your gun really should be on your hip all day, not stuffed in some drawer when you most need it. For easiest packing, I've come to prefer the Colt CCO.

I won't debate the relative merits of auto versus revolver here; each has its merits, and both deserve a place in the collection of the person trained in the use of handguns. Anyone can learn to shoot a handgun well if he has time, desire, and a good supply of ammo. Start with an accurate 22.

Again, spare parts and even spare guns are good ideas. One spare handgun might be in 9mm caliber, since that is the standard military handgun ammo for most of the free world, even though I have no fondness for that cartridge. You might be able to pick up some good supplies of that ammo, and it is prudent to be able to shoot it in one or several handguns.

Along the same lines, it is far more important to know *when* to shoot than to know how to shoot. Try to get some good training at a facility such as Gunsite, or Thunder Ranch, or from traveling instructors like Massad Ayoob or Chuck Taylor. Ayoob does perhaps the best teaching of the aftermath of a potential shooting encounter, and what you need to do for yourself in that sad case. You may consider participating in some serious action-shooting handgun games. The old IPSC matches used to be great for that, but apparently not anymore. Yet any kind of handgun competition will serve you well in the long run. It's all part of shooting under stress, and the more you can get under your belt before you leave the city for the sticks, the better off you'll be.

Give serious thought to how you're going to carry your self-defense handgun in the winter, because you'll be wearing tons of heavy clothing most of the time. I have found a shoulder holster to be one good solution. All it takes to get at the gun is to drop a zipper or pop open some snaps. I used a shoulder holster to carry my K-22 on the trapline for two winters and it was a comfortable and efficient carry. The gun rode warm and dry under my outer garments and was always ready for action.

Some sourdoughs pack their gun outside the clothes in winter. This may be okay if the gun is prepared for the cold and if it's kept outside all the time in cold weather, and you keep the snow and ice off it. But a cold gun will have cold oil, unless you have dealt with that. Also, your bare hand will freeze to the gun as soon as you touch it. I can't shoot a sixgun with gloves on, so I keep my gun warm.

One more thought on sixguns and winter in Alaska. In the sad event that you may have to shoot someone, remember that your opponent will be wearing many layers of bulky clothing through which your bullet must travel before it reaches him. Choose your hand artillery with that in mind.

Fighting shotguns, known as riot guns, may be had in numerous configurations including semiautomatics that look like something out of *Star Trek*. Some of them can be fired with one hand, and that might come in handy. Other riot guns such as the Remington 870 can be fitted with a regular barrel and can then be used as a normal hunting shotgun. Personally I've never been entirely happy with the idea of a convertible gun. It'll always be in the wrong configuration when you want it for something. If you want a riot gun, fine. Keep it as a riot gun and get something else for wing shooting.

One exception I'd permit is a conversion kit to shoot 22 LR in my prime self-defense handgun. To that end I have a Kimber conversion that fits all of my 1911 45 ACP handguns, and it works really well.

Consider your choices of sporting guns and fighting weapons very carefully. They are not inexpensive, so plan ahead. Remember to get guns for everyone, get enough ammo, get spare parts for everything, and get good cleaning equipment for everything.

No matter how remote your retreat it might be a good idea to provide yourself with one or more firearms that can make use of current Russian or Chinese military rifle ammo, most particularly the 30 Russian Short (7.62 x 39). Today, a host of makers can sell you carbines in that caliber. The old SKS is still a good option, though they sell for three times what I paid for one twenty years ago. Ruger also makes—or made—several rifles that take the 30 Russian. Of course the AK-47 is popular, though I personally don't much like 'em.

My personal experience includes plenty of time spent evaluating two versions each of the FAL, HK-91, and M14S or M1A. I prefer my M14S over all other 308 battle rifles because of its excellent setup by Clint McKee of Fulton Armory, and the fact that it has a wood stock (more friendly in the cold) and a very long sighting radius. I have also tested the various AR-10 types by ArmaLite, Rock River, SIG, and a few others, and most of them work just fine. There are lots of choices, so look around, try to shoot before you buy, but be sure to go out and get yours.

Make sure the guns you pick suit you and your family members. Practice with them, and learn how to do simple repairs on them. Get them all sorted out well before you desperately need them. Get your family involved too. Ingenuity and determination set apart the individuals who would choose Alaska over any other retreat location. Careful planning and intelligent choices combined with the resolve to survive result in individuals who are in a very high state of preparedness.

Oddments

Often we hear the phrase, "The silent north." In the dead of winter in interior Alaska it's a most appropriate phrase. One well-known author, when writing about the silence of the far north, went so far as to say the term was inaccurate. He said that the sounds of winter were continuous and ever-changing, implying that there was a lot to listen to in the winter. In my experience, nothing could be farther from the truth.

True, the lakes groan and creak as they freeze, and I'm told the noise of ice on the Yukon during breakup is deafening. From time to time you will hear the call of a wolf pack in the night in the winter. But I have yet to hear the aurora snap and crackle like a sky full of Rice Krispies as some folks would have you believe, and I have seen some pretty good displays. The cabin walls pop and bang, but that's about it for noise.

Take a short walk into the woods when it's 50 below or colder. Stop and stand perfectly still and listen. You will hear absolutely nothing. Not the slightest breath of wind will be blowing, not a branch stirring, the hoarfrost thick on the branches as every last vestige of moisture crystallizes out of the air. Nothing, absolutely nothing, is moving in that killing cold. The loudest sound may very well be the beating of your own heart. Every living thing has found its hole and gone into it to try to survive, to preserve what little degree of warmth it can until the weather breaks. I advise you to do the same.

If you want to warm up quickly when you come in to a warm cabin from the extremely cold outdoors, get your coat off as quickly as you can when you get inside. How often I have seen some chilled person insist on keeping his coat on just a little longer, assuming that if he keeps it on he will warm up faster. Think about it a minute. The outside temperature of your coat is still that of the outdoors even though you are standing inside. It takes time to heat the coat, the insulation of the coat, and finally the wearer of the coat. Might as well let the coat heat up on a hanger while you are getting warm without all that insulation between you and the warm room air. Get the coat off fast and you'll get warm fast.

During the spring, starting at about the end of April, the birds begin to arrive at their breeding grounds. For the rest of the summer the north is anything but silent. From about the middle of May on into the summer the bird life makes big lakes such as Lake Louise a paradise for bird watchers and photographers. The birds all are in their breeding plumage and are going through their various displays and courting motions.

In just one day, without actually trying, just incidental to my outdoor activities I saw the following birds: common and semi-palmated plovers, yellowlegs, white-winged scoters, red-breasted mergansers, red-throated grebes, common and red-breasted loons, trumpeter swans, Canada geese, dippers (ouzels), a bald eagle, a flock of teal, some mallards, and the usual swallows, chickadees, and sparrows that flock around the buildings. If I were a serious bird watcher I could have easily identified twice as many different birds, but I don't have a lot of interest in it. Still, the incredibly varied bird life inspired me to at least have some idea what all those different feathered flappers were.

No bird makes a finer sound to my ear than the loon. He makes different sounds in the spring from those he makes in the fall. In spring his noise is a shrill clarion call. As fall chills the air his call turns mournfully sad. Heard most of the summer and far into the fall, the lonely cry of the loon will get your attention every time you hear him. When the loon cuts loose with his quavering yodel or clarion call, the north woods ring. In sheer volume I think the loon outdoes the trumpeter swan, whose call is deafening at close range. The swans are very loud, but I think the loon is louder. It carries well.

Get a good set of binoculars and keep them handy by the window where you do most of your window-gazing. They will let you see what is going on in the world outside your window throughout the year. I use the 8X32 Leitz Trinovids. In my opinion that is the finest binocular money can buy. The Leitz glasses are very costly and some will think their price is too high. However, if I were to lose mine I would somehow find the money to replace them with an identical pair. In my opinion Leitz optics are the finest glasses money can buy, the finest optics in the world.

Zeiss optics are also very fine. However, I don't like the setup of their controls as well as I like the perfect setup on the Leitz. Swarovski also makes some jim-dandy binoculars, though the ones I've seen are quite bulky.

You get pretty much what you pay for in optics. You'll use your binoculars a lot. Don't cheat yourself out of the very great pleasure of seeing what is to be seen through best-quality binocs.

Another very handy item is a 20-power spotting scope on a good tripod. I use one of the old Bushnell Sentry II spotting scopes. The variable power spotting scopes, such as the old Bausch and Lomb and Redfield, do not have the clarity of optics that my old Bushnell has, but some of today's better spotting scopes may have overcome the variable-optic limitations of twenty years ago. As noted, the optics of fixed-power scopes are generally better than the variables, and you can get replacement eyepieces to raise the power of scopes like the Sentry II. A cheap zoom spotting scope is not worth its cost because the optics are fuzzy. However, an inexpensive fixed-power scope can be a good bargain. Twenty power is enough for many uses, but if your activities include sheep hunting get a 32X or 40X eyepiece as well as the 20X.

Bring a good camera with you and try to get a good long lens for it, something from 300mm on up. During my first three years in the bush I missed a lot of photo opportunities because I didn't own a long lens. Twenty years ago I recommended a good basic SLR with macro lens instead of the normal lens, then some sort of wide-angle like a 24mm, 28mm, or 35mm. Today I'd say get a good digital SLR with a really good zoom from 18-70 mm, would still recommend a macro lens that lets you get really close, and then add the longest high-quality lens you can manage. Get some way to store millions of pix, because even in no-electricity situations you'll want to take photos. Because you can't count on repair services, you'd better have an extra camera body.

Besides the overworked Alaskan pastime of boozing it up, there is the unofficial state sport of lying, of which the newcomer should beware. I think there are more liars per capita in Alaska than anywhere else in the world. Much of the lying is harmless, tall tales told with tongue in cheek by people who don't really expect you to believe them, and in many cases the listener encourages the liar. However, some of the lying is malicious, the liar clearly expecting you to swallow his line as though it were gospel, and daring you to refute him.

Some of the nonsense people have expected me to believe is truly staggering. Many times I've had a hard time keeping a straight face when confronted with the absolute nonsense somebody was trying to pass off as fact. Apparently there is so much missing from some folks' lives that they have to lie in order to compensate for that lack. They have to claim to have done something big in order to make themselves feel important. They're only kidding themselves and those who don't know any better. If you keep your eyes open and your ears tuned, you can usually pick out the bull-throwers from the rest.

One example: A bull-thrower who used to live not too far from me told some gun stories in one of the local bars at Lake Louise one night, and I happened to overhear. I didn't know him at the time, nor anybody else in Alaska for that matter, having just arrived. He told everybody within earshot he knew a lot about guns. I was already a many-times-published gunwriter, a gun collector, a gunsmith, and a student of guns since my childhood. I listened carefully. I heard marvelous tales of exciting new calibers that simply didn't exist (the .428 Westley-Thomson, or the .342 Briggs & Stratton . . . !?). I heard names of famous gunwriters that also didn't exist, and I heard some amazing facts about impossible bullet performance (8,000 fps!), and on and on. Some of the listeners were apparently impressed with his manure, but for those of us who know guns it was a pathetic performance. It was as if a neon sign was flashing over his head, saying, "Liar! Liar!"

One more example: Another fellow, perfectly capable of doing some amazing things in his own right, told me that he had put over 100,000 rounds through one of his revolvers. He showed me the gun. It was obvious that the gun had been carried a lot, but it had not had many rounds fired through it. The firing of 100,000 rounds leaves indelible signs of usage, such as gas cutting on the top strap, erosion on the barrel throat, and battering and looseness here and there. I have fired several thousand rounds through several good sixguns and my experience as a gunsmith tells me what to look for. That guy was simply a bald-faced liar.

If someone wants you to believe he is the local mayor, or owns a certain lodge or airplane or yacht, or that he is responsible for the world being round, you had better take the time and trouble to verify the integrity of the source before you believe it. There is a lot of baloney flying around Alaska.

Breakup

Breakup comes long after you have given up hope of ever seeing a warm spring day again. It starts with the coming of warm air. In a series of cycles the surface of the snow alternately melts and refreezes, leaving a treacherous thin crust on its surface that usually won't quite hold your weight. Snowshoes are useless because the snow's surface is slippery ice, and the snowshoes become big clumsy ice skates. If you break through the crust you sink deep into the rotten snow beneath the surface. Snowmobiles don't work too well on that kind of surface and walking is worse.

Spring breakup brings the ducks. Here is a flock of old-squaws on the edge of the melting pan ice. This is looking south from Army Point toward Evergreen Lodge and Lake Louise Lodge. There's a spring storm coming in from the south.

If you have to drive somewhere in your car, you'll need gallons of windshield washer to clean the muddy grime off your windshield. The snow turns black with splashed mud, then melts and runs with the spring rain into the melting rivers and lakes. The northern world is a mess. However, the feeling in the air at breakup time is a feeling of renewed life that makes all these hardships minor ones. Winter is finally over.

The warm days and the warm air finally dissipate the snow into runoff water. The runoff water flows into the natural drainages of streams and rivers and its warmth melts them, too. So it is that the drainages are the first bodies of water to melt. The lakes melt long afterward.

As the lake shores turn from snow and ice to relatively warm water, the ice of the lake recedes from the shore leaving islands of ice, called pans. Sometimes bridges of ice form across streams and rivers, and these ice bridges can be extremely dangerous.

This past spring two men decided to ride their snowmachines across a raging river on an ice bridge. The bridge was too thin for the combined weight of them and their snowmachines. It gave way, they were swept under the ice by the fast current of water, and they both drowned.

It was the middle of May and I was stuck. All the snow had gone from the ground. In fact it had been gone for more than two weeks. Last year's brown dead grass had not yet permitted the new green shoots to come through, but they were on the way. The ice pan on Lake Louise had receded enough to leave a 100-yard gap around the edge of the lake, so I couldn't go anywhere across the lake with the snowmachine. If I had wanted to go get the mail or make the twenty-mile drive to the nearest phone I'd have had to walk two and a half miles across the muskeg just to get to my car. There was just enough ice around the edge to keep me from getting my boat through, but maybe I could have got through with a canoe. Fortunately, I had a good supply of beans in the larder and didn't really have to go anywhere.

Breakup ice along Knik River near Anchorage.

About four weeks each spring and another four weeks each fall you can't cross a big lake like Lake Louise with either boat or snowmachine. There's either not enough ice or too much. The same conditions exist if you live on the other side of a stream or river from the major access route to your home. Hovercrafts work well on this surface, though. If you live where you have to cross a big body of water to get in and out, plan ahead and have enough supplies to see you through. Get your fuel and food supplies to your retreat cabin during late winter, when it's easy to cross the ice. It's easier to handle fifty-five-gallon drums full of oil or gasoline by sliding them over the ice than it is to lift them in and out of a boat.

Some planning is indicated, depending on where you have your cabin. If you are really remote, accessible only by air, it is a good idea to plan to be "out" by a certain date. Some trappers get flown in to a remote cabin and spend the whole winter gathering their fur, and then head out in the spring to sell it and enjoy life all summer. They might get a job as a fisherman for the summer. Next fall they head back to the bush to do it all over again. They let someone know when they expect to be "out." If they have trouble of some kind, sickness, or an accident and they don't make it out on schedule, somebody will go looking for them.

Glennallen's radio station KCAM broadcasts messages, called "Caribou Clatters," to those who live in the bush. Several other stations throughout Alaska follow suit. An AM radio and good batteries are essential, and of course it's not possible to return the messages. Some sort of radio-phone or two-way radio is needed if you want to talk to the outside world. Most of the families around Lake Louise have citizens band (CB) radios or ship-to-shore high-frequency two-way radios. Some lodges use radio phones or sideband shortwave radio communications. You have to have a generator or other strong source of electrical power if you want to send messages via radio. Transmitting takes lots more power than receiving.

I suspect the prudent retreater would equip himself with a simple continuous wave (CW) shortwave radio that sends and receives Morse code. A simple CW rig should not put too great a strain on the bank account, and power requirements will be somewhat less than needed for voice communication.

How to get in and out if you don't want to walk? If you can't live with the idea of walking in and out during freeze-up and breakup, there are several ways to go. The Weasel is one of the most expensive but most reliable means of access. These look like jeep bodies fitted with tracks instead of wheels. Some of them have cabs, some are open. The new ones have comfortable heated cabs. They can travel over muskeg that'll swallow any ordinary vehicle.

A small vehicle called the "Max" has six fat tires, three per side, and is steered like a dozer: put the brakes on one side's wheels and you turn in that direction. You can fit a track over the wheels to make the Max into a small Weasel.

Some of the other wheeled vehicles that are available, convenient, and useful include three- and four-wheelers. These have big, fat tires, and they are made by Honda and Suzuki, and perhaps others. The four-wheeled versions are a bit safer. A few folks use motorcycles, but they can't carry heavy moose quarters like the three- and four-wheelers can.

Some people use their snowmachines in the summertime. They slip plastic or wood protectors over the skis, or just let them rub on the ground. Those snowmachines that have "bogey" wheels over which the rubber track runs have an easy time in summer conditions. Slide-rail machines can't be used in summer. I suspect that any snowmachine used in summer will suffer from engine overheating.

The problem of year-round access to your retreat can be solved, if you have a long pocketbook, by building a road to your front door. However, by state law you can't prevent anyone else from using your private road to gain access to their land. So if you spend a fortune to make a road five miles into the bush and then someone comes along and acquires a piece of land four miles down the same road, you must let him use your road. Work it out with your neighbors before you build.

Perhaps the ultimate remote cabin access is by air. With an airplane you can get into small lakes in remote areas all over the state and you can't get to them any other way. There are very few roads in Alaska. With planning, you can make sure you can get your airplane in to your cabin site all year-round. If your aircraft is equipped with wheels you can clear a dirt runway for summer, and land in the same place in winter on skis. Or you might prefer to use floats on the airplane in summer. Note that there are lots of airplanes in Alaska, and anyone with a set of wings can drop in whenever he wants to, whether or not you're home.

With the arrival of breakup and the first open water on lakes, the fishing gets marvelous. The lake trout have had a roof of ice over their heads for eight months and they're ready for a change of diet. The fishing is good during breakup and also at freeze-up when the coming winter makes the fish eager to get the last bugs of summer into their bellies.

With the coming of spring all the birds in the world appear in the far north. Trumpeter swans, snow geese, ducks, and songbirds of every description and size all come north to breed and multiply each year. With them come the predatory birds.

My first spring at Lake Louise, the first migratory birds I saw were snow geese. The trumpeter swans also got to the lake early, but right on the heels of the geese were the bald eagles, up from the coast. When I saw the first baldy here at the lake, the lake was still completely covered with ice. Soon, a pocket of open water appeared half a mile north of my cabin. All the birds in the area flocked to that small puddle of water every day, crowding and pushing and shoving and calling each other names. The little pool gradually grew and other pockets of water opened up and the birds spread out into their own territory. When the lakeshore finally thawed, the birds got busy building their nesting sites.

One day the trumpeters started carrying on like a bunch of crazed kids with toy bugles. I grabbed the binoculars and soon located the source of trouble: a big bald eagle sat perched on the shore, watching and waiting. Though they are mostly fish eaters, the bald eagles get their share of ducks.

The bald and golden eagles, the owls, hawks, and falcons kill a great many game birds. The big eagles also take a good number of Dall sheep lambs and other young game animals. The adult trumpeters are not in too much danger from the smaller predatory birds. The trumps can weigh up to thirty pounds, the biggest waterfowl in the world.

As the ice pan on the lake gets smaller and breaks up, a new hazard materializes. The wind blows the ice from one side of the lake to the other, and as it comes across the lake and onto shore it has tremendous momentum. If you leave your dock in the water it can be destroyed by the tons of ice slamming into it. Those who have extensive dockages, such as the owners of the lodges around Lake Louise, try to remove them from the water at the end of summer to avoid their getting destroyed in the spring. Either that or they cut them loose and float them into protected coves so the ice won't destroy them. I've seen the lake ice crumple thick steel plate like so much cardboard. If your dock is in the way, kiss it good-bye.

Lake Louise looking north. The lake has numerous small islands such as the one shown here. On a clear day you could see the Alaska Range, about fifty miles away. The lake can be this calm, or it can kick up four-foot or higher waves.

Lake Louise in an angry mood. This is my old fourteen-foot Chris-Craft boat that I had my second year on the lake. This was taken just after a storm that destroyed Andy and Ruthie Runyan's dock completely, pieces of which are strewn all over the beach. I hauled my boat out of the water and set a big anchor to keep it there, and the boat was unharmed.

Springtime is the time to put away your cold weather gear and break out your hip boots or knee boots. About all you'll need to stay warm in the spring is a light down or synthetic-filled jacket with the standard hat of the north, the wool watch cap. As spring quickly becomes summer, you'll only need your coat early morning and late evening, if then.

Get your boat into shape early. It'll get lots of use during the short summer. Get your boat motor cleaned up and ready to go, and get all your fishing tackle in order during the early spring when you can't do much of anything else that requires walking about, and when you can't do any fishing because of the ice.

Put away your snowmobile with some preventative oil in the cylinders, and stick a board under each ski to keep them from rusting during the summer. Come the first snowfall, they'll still be nice and slick and ready to go.

Spring is also the time to take a walk around your cabin and outbuildings and look for all the little items like tools and traps you dropped in the snow during the winter and couldn't find. If you are a shooter/reloader, check your range for all the brass that you dropped in the snow. It's surprising what turns up in the spring.

The bird watchers go nuts at this time of year. So do those of us who chase big game with a camera. Spring is a great time to spot big-game animals as they change their hangouts. You can often see moose walking the shoreline or making the last trip across the ice to their summer digs. Just the other night a young bull moose snuck by in front of my cabin, not twenty feet away. He was walking in the edge of the water, apparently trying to avoid leaving a scent or leaving tracks. Maybe his feet were hot. Something had disturbed him and he looked annoyed at having to leave his favorite willow patch. Sure enough, next morning he came by again, heading in the opposite direction, back toward his hideout. It is always a surprise to me that something so big can move with so little noise.

While on the subject, I am also amazed how a big animal like a moose can disappear behind the smallest evergreen tree. The dark colors of the moose blend in with the shadows, and you can pass very close by them without seeing them. Good thing they ain't man-eaters! I watched a couple of skiers approach a cow moose one day. I had a vantage point high above the scene and I could see the moose and the skiers clearly. The skiers spotted the moose tracks and looked for the moose. Then they decided not to go through the woods on the moose's trail, which was probably a good idea. Their path would have taken them into the moose's lap. The moose was no more than twenty-five feet away from them and they never saw her.

Looking northwest, with the lake frozen. There is a moose bedded just below the center of the photo, her shoulder hump and head showing above the deep snow. Way out on the lake two cross-country skiers approach, though I doubt they will be visible in the reproduction of this photo. They passed right by this moose and never saw her.

Once I encountered a big bull moose as he stood in an open area covered with the melting snow of early spring. I had just come out of the woods. There were a few small spruce trees scattered throughout the open area. I felt the bull's eyes on me before I saw him, so I started looking for him. I found him about seventy-five yards away, peering over the top of a spruce tree at me as he tried to figure out what I was. He kept behind the tree as I moved along. I "counted coup" on him with the old Watson 450 Express double rifle I was carrying.

The wind was quartering from my left, and I was heading on a path that would take me directly upwind of the bull. I would pass him no more than a hundred yards away. I was curious what he would do when he got my wind. This was an area where lots of people go hiking, and where there are quite a few dogs and more than a few grizzlies. I figured the moose would bolt when he got my wind, but when the big bull finally smelled me he just put his head down and continued to feed. He was quite used to the scent of people, but for all he knew (before he got my scent) I could have been a bear. In that same area I've seen tracks of big grizzlies following the tracks of moose. As soon as the moose got my scent he lost interest in me completely. He knew I meant him no harm.

Once you have made it through the winter, spring will be a very pleasant time indeed. With the coming of spring the days now get longer, about six minutes a day longer on average, which means you get an hour more daylight every ten days. This is most welcome. You'll find you spend more and more of your time out-of-doors as summer comes along, soaking up the much-needed sunlight.

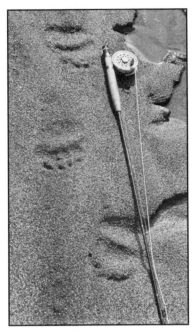

Fresh bear tracks. There are always hazards in Alaska. "Something deadly can come at us at any time."

Spring passes quickly into summer and the days get very warm. Summer temperatures at Lake Louise range from 70 up to 100 degrees, with the average temperature around 75-80 degrees at midday and about 60 at night. This is a bit hotter than a typical Anchorage or coastal day, the temperature near the ocean being regulated by ocean air currents.

Night during the month of June is night by name alone. It is very bright outside at midnight. The sun actually does disappear briefly below the northern horizon during the longest day at Lake Louise, though at Deadhorse on the north slope of the Brooks Range it remains above the horizon all twenty-four hours. At the Lake Louise latitude enough light leaks around the horizon at midnight that you can easily read a newspaper inside your cabin at that darkest hour. The sun describes a large circle overhead, rising in the north-northeast, then moving in a big arc to the south at noon, then taking a very long time to set again in the north-northwest. Sunrise and sunset last a very long time at this time of year because of the slanting path of the sun as it sinks into the horizon. For that matter, sunrise and sunset are quite gradual throughout the year.

The only bad thing about this happy time of year is the presence of bugs, which are probably not as bad as you have heard. At relatively open locations such as Lake Louise the wind often helps keep the mosquitoes and the annoying little no-see-ums and other flying contrivances off of your face and out of your eyes. Anywhere you have standing water and not much breeze you'll have lots of bugs. At some locations the mosquitoes are unbelievable. Yet one of the worst populations of mosquitoes I have seen in my life was in Michigan, where my brother and I once stood back to back and swatted dozens off our arms and bodies with each slap. I have seen mosquitoes just about that bad in Alaska the past few years, when we have had heavy rains. At any rate, modern bug dope works very well. Once in a while you see someone using a head net, but I have never used one.

Tom Main showed me a net coat that you soak in bug dope and then put it over your summer shirt. He says it works quite well to keep the winged pests away, and it lets the cool breeze through at the same time.

Spring and summer are fine and comfortable seasons in Alaska, at least in the south central part of it where I lived. These seasons are the time to get yourself and your equipment in order for the hunting season in the fall, and get set for the next long winter.

And so the ice melts and the brief spring arrives, quickly giving way to summer and the easy life. But watch out . . . winter is fast coming on again!

The cabin in spring with the porch installed. The barrel on the stand holds oil for the heating stove.

Army Point Journal

This chapter consists of a few notes taken from a journal I kept at Army Point. I began an "Alaska Journal" more than a year before I came to Alaska. I kept notes of what I thought I should bring to Alaska, where and how I thought I ought to settle, and of my feelings about leaving civilization behind. The journal also contains notes I made as I drove north on the Alcan Highway into colder and colder country, and some notes of my earliest wanderings in Alaska before I found my cabin on Army Point above Lake Louise in the late fall of 1978. If you're planning to come up for a look around you might want to start a journal of your own. There's no better way to keep track of your thoughts and ideas.

My journal extracts begin here when I had just moved into my cabin on Army Point. With the help of a new friend, Lennie Fitzpatrick, I had finally found a cabin that looked like it could be fixed up to suit me. It was one of several that had been erected by the United States Army many years ago on a point of land overlooking Lake Louise, and then abandoned. The area was called Army Point. The cabin I found there was basically sound, though it needed work here and there to make it livable.

The cabin had no glass in the windows. It had a good plank floor up off the ground about a foot or so. The door was a sheet of plywood. The roof leaked. The walls were made of rows of logs milled flat on three sides. The logs had warped and there were big gaps between them. The logs were about four or five inches thick, and that thickness of wood was the only insulation in the cabin. One of the first things I did was to cover the inner walls with Visqueen to help keep out the cold. I put in a frenzied couple of weeks trying to get the cabin livable before the really cold weather hit, and I got the job done to my minimal satisfaction.

The cabin, first winter. You can tell there's poor insulation in the roof by the grand collection of icicles.

The first friend I made in Alaska, the late Lennie Fitzpatrick, told me where to find my cabin on Army Point. Lennie welcomed me into his house the first day I met him even though he didn't know me from Adam. We sat up well into the night, we drank several pots of coffee, and we talked. Lennie gave me my first education about Alaska. Lennie and his wife Sue and their family went out of their way to help me get settled into my "poached" cabin. Lennie built my first barrel stove, which had a sheet-metal door made from yet another barrel, and that stove kept me very warm all winter long. Lennie's boy Lance came over and helped me from time to time, and was a very great help when it came to scrounging raw materials to make my cabin more of a home.

I was very lucky to find that cabin. Anyone coming to Alaska ought to understand that the Alaskan bush is not dotted with cabins you can just move into when you arrive. There are a few out there, but someone owns them. If you try to "poach" a cabin as I did, you'll most likely get kicked out. You won't endear yourself to Alaskan authorities or to locals. I was both foolish and lucky. I could have been asked to move out at any time. But when the army eventually found out about me and they came out to the lake to investigate, this is what happened. They met me, took a look at how I had very greatly improved the cabin and cleaned up hundreds of pounds of garbage from the locality, and then they told me I could stay there as long as I wanted as unofficial caretaker. Only thing was, I could never own that cabin or the land on which it sat. I had no control over who camped outside my door. That is one reason why, several years later, I moved away.

I moved into my cabin on Army Point on the third of October, 1978. The following notes cover the period from October 1978 to mid-May 1979, my observations on my first winter in the Alaskan bush.

Friday, 6 October 1978

It's still hard to believe I'm not just camped up in the mountains outside Denver. I guess it's because it all took place rather fast. Put a major move like this off long enough and then finally make the move, and it seems like it all happens in a rush. One day I'm taking a shower in a nice house in Denver and the next I'm bathing with lake water in a little cabin deep in the heart of Alaska.

Lennie Fitzpatrick made me a lovely barrel stove yesterday with his welding and cutting torch. Somehow it seems to be cheating to use things such as power tools out here but they do get the job done.

Lunch is about over and I must get the stove installed, and I promised Len I'd help him pound nails on his garage today in exchange for his work on the stove. Besides, the little mouse here is waiting for a warm house. It only took him two days to sink his teeth into my cookies. One needs tight containers for food out here. Flour, cookies, sugar, salt, beans, coffee, rice . . . are just some of the things to keep boxed up tight against rain and critters. *[What I thought were mice turned out to be voles.]*

Saturday, 7 October

I worked hard yesterday to get the stove installed and the roof sealed. Fitz and his boy came over to see why I hadn't come to their house to help them work. I was still playing with the roof then, after dark, using putty to try and seal all the cracks. It rained today and I found out from the fresh damp spots that the roof is not yet sealed.

The author is patching the leaks around the "homburg" made from half a fifty-five-gallon barrel. This kept out the rain, kept the hot pipe away from the roof, and kept the smokestack nicely in place. This stack was originally not high enough, but in this photo you see the final height, which was tall enough.

I spent today at Fitz's helping build his garage. Before I went over there I got up very stiff and sore and gave myself a bath, a haircut, and shampoo. Felt pretty good. Had a headache on awakening from my first night with the stove burning. Must have been the paint on the stove burning off.

Fitz came with his boy last night and we finished disassembly of the big table, which was in the way of the stove. His boy Lance pulled a lot of nails and did some good work for me. We then put up the stack and top-hat and fired up the stove for the first time. We had quite a time getting the fire to burn that first time, but burn it did, and heated up the old paint on the fifty-five-gallon drum, and it stunk to high heaven.

The Fitzpatricks went home about 11:00 P.M. and I went to bed. My fire burned low at 4:30 A.M. and I had to start a new fire with more wet birch. I really stacked in the wood, five big logs, and after about forty-five minutes got a good blaze. I lay shivering in my sleeping bag waiting for the wood to finally catch hold and burn. It was pretty chilly. Once the logs caught I stopped the entire stove down and just let the draft around the leaky door and damper take over. That "set" lasted till past 10:00 this morn, some five hours.

My little stack of wood outside the door turned out to be a two-day supply. I will need about 180 days' worth, so the wood gathering begins tomorrow in earnest.

Jobs for tomorrow: Roof on potty, and tack up the tar paper in there; fix leaks on cabin roof . . . urgent! Gather firewood . . . URGENT! Split kindling. I can store my building materials in cabin #2 *[another cabin near mine]*. Gather more building wood for porch, cabinets, kitchen, and work table, and reloading bench; build doorjamb, re-hang and secure door, etc.

[I picked what I thought was the best of three cabins situated along the top of my hill. I may have been wrong, but I made do okay. One will note there was no shortage of odd jobs to be done. The door, for instance, took three days.]

Me chinking the walls with borrowed insulation, rags, etc.

A couple of kids drove by the cabin today snooping. As a result I rigged up a temporary lock on the door. Fitz suggested shutters for the windows with bar locks to secure the windows when I leave the cabin. He also suggested a concealed latchstring for the door. Both seem good ideas. Kind of too bad I was so lucky to find a place I could drive right up to. This means everyone else can do so also. Still have to drive twenty miles to the postbox, the mailman doesn't come any closer. That's also the closest telephone. *[This has changed. The mailman now drives the twenty miles down to the lake and there are a few phones, both tremendous conveniences for Lake Louise dwellers.]* The nearest grocery is in Glennallen, fifty miles from here, but at least there is a good road all the way. I guess this is remote enough and I shouldn't complain. Can't have everything, not at these prices, I guess!

Sunday, 8 October

What a wild noise, the call of the loon! The song of the wilderness! If I ever take his call for granted I'll move back to the city. Although I had never heard one, the first time one gave its peculiar lonesome cry I knew exactly what it was. It was about a quarter mile or more north of my cabin out in the lake. The day was cloudy (as usual) and wet, and very still.

Sounds can travel mighty far under these conditions. I could clearly hear and understand two boaters talking with each other way out on the lake beyond the loon. One of them asked the other what it was that made that strange sound.

There are many critters around here. Most mornings a magpie runs and scratches and hops across my roof. A squirrel lives in the evergreen just outside my front door. There has not been a day since I moved in five days ago that ducks haven't flown right over the cabin, making me regret time and again that I didn't bring a shotgun.

Every critter seems to grow extra large out here. Foxes are the size of Colorado coyotes. Wolves can weigh over 200 pounds. The magpies are far larger than Colorado crows, and the ravens . . . ! I saw a fishing lure at Fitz's that was about six inches long and had one big treble hook with about 5/8-inch between each shank and point. I asked what manner of whale you hunt with that beastie and was told, "Lake trout." I was also told you string that artificial pike up behind some twenty to thirty inches of steel leader so Mr. Trout doesn't bite through it. Yes, the critters do take on some size in Alaska.

It took me thirty-five minutes to drop my first dead tree, cut it into thirds, and carry the pieces to the cabin. That was over an hour ago and I'm still recovering! Boy, did I ever get soft in the city! Well, one of the reasons I came up here was to get strong and healthy. I'm eating like a horse and have some doubts about my food supply. I'm eating about twice as much as I ate in Denver. I must get my fishing license as soon as possible. Fish and beans is mighty good food.

Last night it got too hot in here. I put on about six or seven green logs at midnight to try and make dawn. At 2:00 A.M. they were mostly gone, even with draft and damper shut tight. Temperature was close to 70 or 80 degrees in here, and the cabin was very comfortably warm when I got up. The little water kettle was boiling away on top of the stove and it was very dry in here. In fact I had a nosebleed. A big jug of water to perk on top of the barrel stove would be a very good idea.

Today I fired my first shots in Alaska. I made a little test with my 22 rifle, the custom Winchester 69A. I shot one shot each of standard velocity, hollow-point, high-speed solid, and "Stinger" ammo to see which hit highest in the lake at about 200 yards downhill. The Stinger won and was also loudest.

My muscles are so sore I could cry. I cut up two more downed trees and brought them to the cabin. Then I went at the cabin roof, after tacking up the tar paper in the outhouse wall and dismantling the "picnic table" in the yard to get some wood for the outhouse roof. The roof of the cabin leaked last night during a steady rain and I plotted the leaks and hope I now have 'em fixed. The entire roof needs to be redone.

Another of my wild friends was this little red squirrel, a gentle female who lived "upstairs," above the ceiling over my head, all winter. These little critters have a language all their own—spoken with their eyes—that can be learned if one is interested. She was good company. Here she's eating peanut butter off a cracker.

Monday, 9 October

I don't like getting up to a cold cabin. I also don't like getting up in the middle of the night to re-stoke my fire so I'll have heat in the morning. Therefore I'm experimenting with log-sets to see how long I can make my stove burn. Some sort of auxiliary heater, such as kerosene or diesel fuel, would be okay, set to burn on "low" all night near the bed. *[Note that this, my first barrel stove, did not have the capability of entirely shutting off the air supply. When I finally got a stove with a good cast-iron door I could make it burn about 50 percent longer than I ever could this one . . . about six hours, up to nearly eight, depending on wood quality.]*

Tuesday, 10 October

This morning was quite special. I saw my first bald eagle today, not fifty yards away sitting in the top of an evergreen looking at me. Suddenly I realized I'm not in Denver!

[I was extremely lucky to have found lots of scrap lumber inside the cabin when I moved in, for which I am very thankful to whatever providence left it there. From it I was able to make some fine shelves, build a thoroughly solid front door, etc. The cabin was furnished with an old spring bed and some crude benches, plus a big built-in table and two smaller loose tables. In addition, there were six shelves build onto the wall around the corner near my bed. There was a poorly-hung door and torn Visqueen on the three small windows. I tore down everything that was on the walls and used the raw materials for rebuilding or for constructing other items. I made a little box to hold kindling, for example. Anything I installed, all the tables, shelves, and the like, had to be able to support my weight or I didn't consider it rugged enough.]

Last night I tightened the springs on the bed, a vast improvement. I also dismantled the big table. The cabin is still cluttered with the two smaller tables and the junk benches. I now have made a design for the inside of the cabin and can get going on it.

Fitz's boy Lance came by and told me how much they had got done at their house. I showed him how little I had got done because I had to do all my woodcutting, cooking, and cleaning up by myself. It was easy to see the benefits of two people working and a third cooking!

What a relief! I just ate dinner, consisting of rice, spinach, and ptarmigan, the first fresh meat I've eaten since leaving Denver! Nearly a month without fresh meat. I ate everything but the beak, feathers, feet, and guts, really relished that bird. Very tasty and much needed! The whole world looks better after such a fine meal.

I have my door nearly done, and it is five and a quarter inches thick. It ought to work okay, and seeing some progress helps my mood. I'm glad my late father isn't here to see what a cobbled-up job I did on it. I am a bit embarrassed about the quality of my work, but in my defense I was working in the dark and working way past the point of exhaustion. In fact, my hand gets so sore from pounding nails that I can hardly make a fist, and to write in this journal is actually painful, the ache of today's work extending up my arm to just short of my elbow.

I'm chiseling the cabin doorway for hinges to hang my new homemade door. This was very early in my stay at Army Point.

The completed door, "Ray's Hell-for-Stout Door." This shows the inside latch, the handle for closing, its latchstring, and its heavy construction. This door weighed well over 100 pounds, and was secured with a hidden latchstring, an optional padlock, and with a hidden steel bolt.

Friday, 13 October

What a fine day! Just one helluva blow last night with some snow, world all white now. Door is done and works well. I do not yet have a lock worked out, just the massive bar across the inside. Door is hell for stout!

Today I'll go to town (Glennallen) to get food and hang my mailbox out by the main highway.

Saturday, 14 October

Got my mailbox up yesterday and bought food in town. I spent my last dollar yesterday, so now it's up to the mailbox and the people who owe me money for my writing and photos.

Sunday, 15 October

Very tired today after an exhausting day of work Saturday. I got a chill fiddling around on the roof with regular socks and low shoes on. Mistake! By nightfall I'd gathered and cut a lot of firewood, but a breeze sprang up from the west, whistling through the walls of my cabin like they were made of cheesecloth. Consequently, though I was very tired even after I ate a mess of beans and my corn leadcakes (a culinary delight!), I felt compelled to tack up some Visqueen onto the west wall. This I did, and when I finished, the thin plastic sheeting ballooned out away from the wall from the wind. I need to get some batting on it to keep it in place. It does seem to keep it warmer in here, though. It was late when I finished, and man, was I beat! I went to bed thinking I'd freeze since it was both cold and blowing outside. It was 10 to 20 degrees above zero outside *[Fahrenheit, as are all temperatures mentioned in this book]*, not all that cold, but with a stiff breeze blowing the chill factor was probably well below zero. I woke an hour after I hit the sack and I was running sweat. My good old Eddie Bauer down sleeping bag really does its stuff!

Today I fired my 470 Churchill double rifle out over the lake to get the neighbors used to the rolling thunder that will be associated with my house on the hill. So far no complaints. Try that in downtown Denver!

Here's the completed front porch, made from timbers robbed from another of the abandoned cabins on Army Point. This is looking northwest, with a corner of the lake in the background.

I also got some rug scraps today and put them on the floor for insulation. The scraps just about cover the open area of the floor. The place is starting to look civilized. The rug scraps seem to help insulate a bit. Sure wish I had a wood cookstove.

Monday, 16 October

Hauled water . . . some thirty gallons of it, all the way 200 yards up the road from the lake. This is about sixty feet vertically from the lake.

Last night a little owl came to greet me with silent flight and a swoop, as I stood staring at the stars at the corner of my cabin. There was a full moon up. Little Owl sat in one of my spruces outside the door and looked at me in unafraid curiosity. I spoke to him in gentle tones. He was only some six to eight inches long in body. He seemed all head. I could only see his silhouette and as I opened the cabin door to get a better look at him the latch banged down and off he flew. But he seemed to be completely unafraid. I felt if I'd held out my hand he would have come to sit on it. But I was well aware of sharp talons and beak and I wasn't wearing gloves, so I didn't try. I wished him good hunting as he flew off.

Wednesday, 18 October

I had a good day yesterday and got up some insulation in the roof to chink in a few of the holes there. The insulation came from an old Quonset hut I found abandoned and falling down near here. It cost me only a face-full of dust to collect it.

It is getting warmer day by day, it seems. Today for the second time in a row it's been above freezing. The lull before the storm?

Last night I played my old five-string Gibson banjo for the first time in the cabin. Nothing rings like a Gibson! *[My banjo was a Gibson RB-150 bowtie from about 1950.]*

Thursday, 19 October

A beautiful quiet crisp morn. I take my coffee black, strong, made on the barrel stove, and outside. Crisp fall mornings like this are incredibly beautiful, truly the stuff of life. I couldn't sleep, so I got up, put on the pot, got to my woodcutting, and now enjoy a quiet moment with pen.

I went to Fitz's today and gave him the hide off a muskrat I had shot and he showed me how they are supposed to be skinned out. He also told me there was a grizzly prowling around last night, which might have been what made me so restless. His boy saw it some weeks back, and a couple of dogs in the neighborhood raised holy hell last night, so maybe that was the problem with my sleep. Another fellow saw its track on the road near here and confirmed it to be a grizzly.

I got a window pane on one of the windows, the one looking northwest toward the lake. I found a good piece of Plexiglas and used that. I put it in the bottom half of the window opening with the two layers of Visqueen on the top half. Now I can look out the window while sitting down by it.

Lake Louise looking northwest, the view from my cabin window. The lake is just beginning to freeze as shown by the dark/light patches on the surface. The little cabin down by the docks in the right center of the photo furnished the overhead ceiling wood for the cabin and also the wood for my front porch.

Saturday, 21 October

Yesterday I put up a washstand made out of the solid oak table I found here. I also got my gun rack up. Then I built my kitchen table out of a door I found that must weigh 100 pounds, into one corner of the cabin. It is mounted high enough so I can work comfortably on top of it while standing in front of it. The height is perfect, but I'd like more countertop room.

Today I'll try to get my desk and reloading table installed, but first I must haul wood and some water, and get to some more of my chinking.

The last two days saw a lot of change in my attitude. Talk of the grizzly make me carry my big 470 double rifle on my back while cutting wood and doing other chores. I suppose I'm overreacting. *[No I wasn't, as I found out a couple years later when a grizzly sow and yearling cub walked right past my cabin while I was in it, in broad day-light.]* I must look like a fool to a lot of folks. I don't yet have my sixguns up here; if I did I'd wear one of them all the time. On the other hand, I would really look like a fool if I was all chewed up by a bear because I had left my rifle home.

[Canadian Customs would not let me bring my handguns across the border, so I arranged to have them shipped to me after I settled in Alaska. I arranged with a firearms dealer to receive them for me in Alaska. The 470 was the only centerfire rifle I had with a sling on it at the time.]

A fellow lake dweller talked me into putting in a reserve oil heater. It seems like I'm giving up something by putting in oil heat, but it will save time. I'm now spending all my time collecting wood for the barrel stove. It seems like I spend all day cutting just enough wood to last through the night. In other words, I can't keep up with my woodcutting. I hope the oil heater will let me catch up.

[I was, at this time, starting to really dread the cold that I was sure was coming. There are notes in my journal to this effect, and it appears to me now I was pretty "chicken" back then. Here are some of those indications:]

. . . I managed to survive pretty well at 10 degrees or less. I guessed the temp at 30 to 35 degrees, and it was actually only 15 . . . I drove a snowmobile at forty miles per hour with no face mask and didn't feel at all cold all day (at 15 degrees temperature). . . . With the windchill factor here it's probably below zero now at the cabin and it's really nice inside.

I heard some wolves yesterday to the west of the cabin. Hope they stay over there.

[On wolves: Several years later, I was running my trapline and ran out of gas five miles from home. I walked those five miles through deep snow in the dark, all the while listening to a pack of wolves steadily drawing closer to me. As they drew nearer I walked faster. Finally they quit calling to each other. I knew they were then on a trail that paralleled the trail on which I was walking and which was less than a hundred yards away. (Don't ask how I knew they were there, I just knew. I proved it to myself the next day when I drove that parallel trail and saw their tracks.) When they stopped howling I wasn't sure what to do, so just kept walking. I didn't hear them again or see them. However, there isn't the slightest doubt in my mind that they knew I was there and had come to see what sort of creature I was, which is to say, to see if I was edible. I don't know or care what you may have heard about whether or not wolves attack man, but I can tell you they got my undivided attention for several hours that night. I didn't feel the least bit secure, though I was armed.]

The wolves in Alaska get sizeable.

Sunday, 29 October

I started a batch of sourdough today. Hope it fares better than the last ill-fated batch I made up a few years ago that just sat there and rotted and stank.

I ate a duck and two ptarmigan. The little duck was just superb, roasted for about two hours in my frying pan. I sure enjoy the wild food! But tonight I overate. I made up a rice-onion-sowbelly-tomato combination that filled my ten-inch frying pan to the top and I ate it all.

Tried out my reloading bench setup today, and it is sturdy and worked just fine. I loaded twenty rounds for the 338 OKH and fired 'em. Nice rifle.

Wednesday, 1 November

Yesterday I paid an accidental return visit to Mr. Owl. I think it was the same critter who came by my cabin one night two weeks ago. I had just cut down two small trees and halved 'em for firewood when I happened to look up. There, not five feet from where I stood, sat this little owl staring at me with his round yellow eyes. He continued to sit there while I went to get the camera and took some pix. I was able to approach him easily to within five feet and hope to have some good pictures.

One of the benefits to my life in the wilderness was the closeness I had with the wild creatures of the woods. This is a boreal owl, about eight or nine inches long.

Thursday, 2 November

My sourdough bread is a fabulous success! I cooked three loaves in the barrel stove, good coals a-blazing, and it came out just perfect. Hallelujah! I'll celebrate by eating another duck sandwich. It was a joy to cut into that first loaf. It looked and tasted just great. I knew I'd put that bacon grease I brought from Denver to good use!

It's very quiet in the deep north in the winter. Absolutely no noise is to be heard once you get away from the human dwelling areas. The animals don't make a sound, unlike the critters on *Grizzly Adams*, where every animal is screaming and bellowing and growling every time its face is flashed on the TV screen. In real life the critters don't advertise their presence. The predator doesn't want the prey to know of his existence and the prey certainly doesn't run around shouting, "Here I am . . . free eats!"

Because it is so quiet in the bush, the slightest odd noise is a warning that something is not quite right. The odd noise really grabs your attention whether you're asleep or awake. You come to really like the quiet.

I saw a hawk owl today flying down the road past the cabin. Saw fox tracks down by the lake today.

Friday, 3 November

I am observing an American Hawk Owl (*Surnia ulula caparoch*) outside my window. He is about sixteen inches long, three-foot wingspan.

[Much later in the year this owl cost me a great deal of grief. He decimated the ptarmigan and they became very spooky. I could not get a shot at them when I badly needed some food late in the winter. I saw little mounds of feathers all over the hill around my cabin, and bits and pieces of half-eaten ptarmigan that the owl had killed.]

Today I ate a small loaf of sourdough bread with marmalade for breakfast. Then I had somewhat over a pint of vegetable soup with half another small loaf of bread and more marmalade for lunch. For dinner I ate the rest of the duck on the last of the sourdough bread, then a mess of fried cornmeal mush and a taste of my new bean-pot. All this was washed down with about five cups of instant coffee, one laced with sugar for quick energy to go and cut wood. I'm still hungry!

Sunday, 5 November

Today I was privileged to watch a mating dance by two bald eagles away out on the thin ice off the next point of land. They seemed to be very wary. I watched from the comfort of my cabin with 20-power spotting scope. The dance showed me where many Indian dance movements came from, the big birds prancing around for all the world as thought they were on hot coals, with wings just slightly spread so you could see the full length of their legs, bodies bent somewhat forward. Both birds did this.

Occasionally one or the other would raise its wings like a duck and make little flapping motions near the top of the wing's arc. Both birds would stand facing in the same direction (north) and then one would sidle up to the other, sidestepping as though to do the popular "bump" dance. I observed (as well as I could tell at that distance . . . about half a mile) the male mount the female after she flapped her wings in the above manner. The dancing and displaying continued some time after mating. About three-fourths of their time together on the ice was spent standing parallel with each other and observing the surroundings as though looking for danger, the bodies being motion-less. One-fourth of the time was spent displaying. About thirty seconds to one and a half minutes elapsed between display cycles.

The two birds mated, then continued displaying for some time. Abruptly one of the birds took wing and flew straight off toward the northeast across the lake, leaving the other bird alone on the ice. Eventually bird number two flew off.

All this took place just before a snowstorm came in from the north.

I got a setline in for fish today, just off the north point of land above my cabin at the tip of Army Point. I scared myself when my axe, probing in front of me with a stout whack every step, went sailing through the ice. I estimate there is about six to eight feet of water under just two inches of ice at that spot.

Thursday, 9 November

I'm becoming increasingly distressed with the vast amount of smoke that escapes into the room every time I load wood into my barrel stove. Lennie Fitzpatrick's advice to use an eight-inch diameter stove-pipe seems like sound advice now, because my six-incher is plugged with wood tar (creosote). Last night the stove tried to choke me out.

I put in a large batch of birch hoping it would flame up okay and stop smoking. It flared up okay, but by then the cabin was filled with smoke. The flaming of the wood did nothing but add to the mess and I had to open the door of the cabin wide at 2:30 A.M., temperature about 20 below zero outside, and air the cabin out. Boy, did I cuss!

I'm getting the false ceiling in place. I have it about one-quarter done and it really cheers up the place.

[The cabin had a ceiling the height of the gable, about fifteen feet above the floor. It was hot as the dickens up in the rafters, and freezing near the floor. The heat loss was terrific through the thin boards of the un-insulated roof. I was putting a dropped ceiling just above the rafters at a height of seven feet above the floor. The idea of the ceiling was to get the warm air to stop rising at the seven-foot level, in effect trap the hot air at a level where it would do me some good. The dead air between the ceiling and the roof acted as insulation. This was a vast improvement, one of the most important things I did to "winterize" the cabin. Another important improvement was covering the walls on the inside with Visqueen as a vapor and heat barrier.]

Yesterday Lance Fitzpatrick and I worked outside for about three hours tearing down the old boathouse down by the lake to get planks for my ceiling and porch. I paid him four boxes of 22 LR. ammo for his work and we were both well satisfied. Now I have building materials and nails for the above jobs, plus wood for shelves, etc.

Even though yesterday was one of the coldest I've seen in years it was so clear and clean it was actually quite pleasant. I could see all the mountain ranges around here.

Some of the strangest sounds are made by the ice as it creaks and groans with an unearthly penetrating sound as it freezes, cracks, and refreezes. This is most prominent when it is extremely cold, as it was yesterday.

Man, am I tired after yesterday's exertions! I'm trying to get the ceiling done today before I go to bed and my limbs ache and refuse to respond. Oh, for some GOOD FOOD! Hope to get some cash in the mail so I can get oil heat in here and some cheap lights. I'm almost out of white gas now for my Coleman lamp.

I checked my setline today for fish, and Lo! I had caught a burbot! This critter was 27-1/2 inches long, the biggest fish I've ever caught.

Friday, 10 November

Sourdough bread again a success! This is my best loaf so far. Birch is mandatory for cooking. I spent five hours today screwing with the stove and never really got the chill out of the cabin. The plan seems to be dry birch only and not very much at a time. One small log about one-and-a-half feet long by three inches diameter keeps it quite warm in here, even when it's about 20 below outside. I am getting the ceiling in, and it must be doing some good.

Late last night, long after dinner and long past the point of exhaustion that precluded any more significant effort for the day, I noticed the temperature was dropping in the cabin. Just that afternoon I had blasted out all the sludge in the stove, so I thought, by building up a good blaze and opening the door and letting the fire roar and rip and burn out all the creosote in the firebox and stovepipe. The room had filled with smoke when I had the door open, but then it cleared up and burned clean, and the room got good and warm. I was quite sure the stove and pipe were clear and functioning properly. That evening when I felt it getting cold again I thought that all I had to do was add more fuel to the fire. I tossed on a log, feeling sure the stove would vent properly. Not so. The room again filled with smoke.

Again I opened the stove door and, to get rid of the smoke, I also opened the cabin door to the 20-below air outside, and instantly had flame and heat. Clearly something was wrong with my stove.

I saw that the ashes had piled up in the bottom of my stove until there was very little room for wood. Aha, I thought, all those ashes must be the problem. Let's get the ashes out of the stove! I proceeded to remove five buckets of ashes from the firebox past the roaring blaze therein, burning my hands and face and covering everything in the cabin with a thick layer of ash. This did absolutely nothing for my stove . . . nor for my temper! By this time I was freezing from the open cabin door, burned from the searing heat of the stove, coughing from the ash in the air, tired as hell, and not at all happy. I was also loudly painting the air a bright shade of blue with my language.

Slowly, very slowly, it started to sink in to my fatigue-numbed brain that whenever I shut the firebox door the roaring blaze immediately quit. It slowly became apparent to me that this indicated there was absolutely no draft up the chimney. The air vent in my stove door was wide open, so there should have been a good draft into the stove and up the chimney. There was none. When I shut the door, smoke poured out around the door and through the air vent in the door. (It must have been obvious, you will say, that if the smoke was not going up the chimney the chimney must have been plugged. That is obvious to me now. It was less than obvious when it was 20 below zero out, I was very cold and tired, and it had never happened before with that stove.)

I realized the pipe must be plugged, but it was pitch-dark out. What to do? I decided to make it through the night by wearing heavy clothes and lots of covers. I would let the fire die out overnight so I could work on the pipe first thing in the morning. That was my intention, but it got so cold (it was minus 20 outside) I had to try to burn some wood for heat, which of course didn't work, and I filled my lungs with smoke all night. I awoke at dawn cold and sore-chested and with a very sore nose from its running from the smoke all night. At any rate I had slept a bit. I went right to work on the chimney.

The chimney was plugged solid with creosote for about two feet in the very top section. I tried to shove my hammer down through the crud but I could not, even when I rammed it down into the soot with all my strength. Accordingly, I disassembled the entire stovepipe and cleaned it thoroughly with a 2x4 and lots of cussing. When I put it back in place I added another two-foot section to raise the pipe and improve the draft. Then I fired up my stove.

I got a helluva blaze in very short order, and the stove is now perfectly functional again. In fact, it works better than ever. I used to huddle right next to the stove to get warm, but now I can't get near it. It's back to school again to learn how to stoke this new setup for maximum effect. I have to relearn how to stoke it with the different types of wood, and relearn how to set the damper and draft. I also *must* clean the pipe at least once a month, preferably every two weeks.

[The pipe never clogged again. I think the added two-foot length was the biggest improvement. I found an easy way to clean the pipe. I used my old Daisy Model 25 BB gun to rap on the pipe where it protruded above the roof. This dislodged the soot, and I didn't have to disassemble the pipe ever again.]

Tuesday, 21 November

I began heating with oil Sunday night the 19th. I sweated all night long the first night because I had both stoves going. My down sleeping bag is too hot. Last night I ran the oil heater on "low" and had an auxiliary fire in the woodstove, but the wood fire burned out during the night. I awoke after ten hours in the sack. I needed all that sleep because I wasn't feeling up to par for some reason. The cabin was chilly, but a twist of the oil control valve had the cabin hot quickly.

A few days ago, before I installed the oil stove, I received an overdue check from one of my clients. I went to Glennallen to get food. On the way home I stopped at Bill Poe's house and we talked guns and hunting until 1:15 A.M. When I got back to my cabin the wind was blowing about 40–50 mph past the door, a steady hard blow that lasted all night. The outside temperature was about 10 below, and because I had no way to keep the cabin warm while I was gone, the temperature inside the cabin was also 10 below. It took me until 4:15 A.M. to get the cabin warm.

Last Friday I made the 200-mile drive to Anchorage to pick up my sixguns, which Denver gunsmith Don Fisher had shipped to me. Driving out the Lake Louise road on the way to Anchorage I saw a small band of caribou. They were beauties, the first I've ever seen. Also saw a moose, and I was again impressed with the incredible size of these animals.

Me in the cabin after having lived there several weeks. I had just received the shipment of my sixguns from Don Fisher. I'm holding my nickel 6-1/2-inch Smith & Wesson M29. Note the improvements to the cabin in the form of the kitchen table in the corner, Visqueen on all the walls, the false ceiling that kept the heat down where it did me some good, and a few scrounged throw rugs on the floor to help keep out the cold. Also, the shelves are done properly, my reloading press is installed, and the coffee-pot is on the little stove. I'm settled in for the winter.

Anchorage was having a cold spell, but nothing like the 37 below we had at the lake when I left. My car started very easily in that cold, but it took both hands to move the gearshift lever.

[I didn't have any sort of block heater in my car. Most of these require electricity, though some run on gasoline or diesel fuel. Basically if your car has sat in extreme cold for a long time, like overnight at 40 below, it will not start unless you're really lucky or unless you apply some sort of heat. Aircraft operating in extreme cold weather in Alaska are generally heated via some sort of propane fire directed at ducting to keep the flame off the engine while the heat is directed there, and there's usually an insulating blanket over the top of the cowling. A similar setup might get your car going. Other good ideas: have a top-quality battery in good condition, i.e., not too old, and keep the oil clean and of the recommended viscosity for extreme-cold conditions. Generally, you're better off relying on your snowmobile for winter travel.]

While I was in Anchorage I took a stroll along Fourth Ave., notorious for its bars and pawn shops and all that attend them. I was walking along peacefully when suddenly a drunken woman came rolling out of the front door of one of the bars, right in front of me. She tumbled end over end across the sidewalk down toward the gutter. She had apparently overstayed her welcome in that particular bar and had been forcibly ejected. She got up, dusted off a few of the bigger chunks of dirt, and tottered off down the avenue toward the next bar. She acted as if nothing had happened, all part of her daily routine. I was suddenly very anxious to get home to my little cabin, and made tracks hastily in that direction.

(Back at the cabin.) We have had temps of 8 to 10 above for the past few days and it is welcome warm weather.

I bought a kerosene lamp for the cabin. It gives quiet illumination instead of the incessant hissing of the Coleman lamp . . . though not nearly so bright.

Sunday night, 10 December

I just enjoyed two lovely hours of silence in the Alaskan bush. I took a nice little sundown walk that took me west across the lake on one of the snowmachine tracks, past the wreckage of an old lodge and up onto the Lake Louise road. I walked down the road to the west, away from my cabin, a half mile or more until I realized the moon was not going to come out to light my way home. I retraced my steps in the gathering gloom, stumbling along the road. When I got home I lit the barrel stove, put it on "high" and got out Jim Beam to help revive myself with some artificial internal warmth. A very pleasant two hours of peace and self-confrontation.

Thursday, 14 December

I don't really want to fumble through another winter up here. Too damned dark. This is for the birds . . . especially owls.

Saturday, 16 December

Today I saw minus 25 most of the day on my thermometer outside the door. Got water today and noticed it is much colder on the lake than here by the cabin.

I got in some wood to heat the cabin because I was going through oil in high style. I like the woodstove better than the oil stove because the heat is closer to the floor, and I enjoy sitting near the warmth, which I can't do with the oil stove.

Still one week to go to the beginning of winter and the shortest day of the year. The sun is sort of up by 9:00 A.M. and mostly gone by about 3:00 P.M. That means eighteen hours of darkness. The darkness is probably the one factor of Alaskan life I was not prepared for, and several times it has depressed me severely.

At 9:10 P.M. it is 33 degrees below zero outside my front door. Lance was just here and he said it is 45 below at his house. The air in my nose was fresh and sharp and felt crystal clear and clean, like a breath from a chilled oxygen bottle. Very definitely very brisk outside. Warm as toast in here.

Sunday night, 17 December

It is now minus 5 outside at 9:30 P.M. I kept my wood fire going all day again to conserve oil. I keep the oil heater on low and the wood gets it as hot as one would ever want in here.

Monday, 18 December

Noon. Dearie me, the wind almost never blows here but when it does it really makes up for lost time. It started gently from the south and then picked up speed and swung around to the west and is now blowing out of the north at 20 mph at least, gusting to 50 mph or better. Unfortunately, I must now venture forth for a necessary short walk to the little building across the road.

I'm back. Lord! The wind is now blasting at a good 50 mph across the top of the hill here. When I opened my big heavy front door the wind whipped it wide open and slammed it against the wall like so much tissue paper, and I was jerked right out of the cabin along with it. It was a damned good push to close it again. The wind is really blowing on Lake Louise!

The other day when it was so cold and I was down on the lake I saw one of the most incredibly beautiful scenes I've ever seen. Looking south toward the sun there was a circular rainbow or halo around the sun, visible on both sides of it in the little bit of ice fog on the surface of the lake. I later found out these light circles are known as sun dogs. Looking north everything was crystal clear and white from direct sunlight, and there was a trace of magenta in the distant sky that shaded to indigo near the horizon. Directly overhead the sky was a deep blue, clean and pure beyond description. The scene was so beautiful it was unreal, with a picture book quality.

Christmas Day, about 25 below zero, it was a good clear day for a walk with the camera. This was my first Christmas at Lake Louise. The sun is about as high as it got that day, barely visible above the horizon to the south, which is to the right in this photo.

Wednesday, 27 December

I had a couple of Christmas moose in the backyard for a few days. They were welcome friends, momma and kiddie. *[They stayed near my cabin for most of the winter. I assume they felt safe there.]*

The moose are very dark brown or black on the bottom and have the appearance of being wet. On top the black shades to brown and becomes quite light on some individuals. The first and most lasting impression one gets of the Alaskan moose is of their massive size and strength.

Ptarmigan are savage eaters. They bite big chunks off the ends of the willow branches along with the buds. I watched one of these birds eat. He put on a grand demonstration of poor table manners, twisting his head this way and that, lashing out with his black beak to snag one bud after another. Once in a while I could see his eyes go shut as he bit off some tough part of the branch. He nearly choked once when he bit off too much.

These birds are great fun to watch when they are trying to balance on a branch that is not quite strong enough to hold them. They flap their tails up and down and their feathered feet scratch for traction, then as the branch gives way they tumble down onto a fellow bird on their way to the ground. They are like a bunch of clowns when a flock of them attacks a willow bush together. They swarm and cackle and burble and flap and crunch, and you can hear them breaking branches and enjoying themselves a long way off.

If, however, the ptarmigan sense that you are hunting them you'll be hard-pressed to see them even if you're staring right at their location. They make absolutely no sound or motion to give away their presence.

Friday, 9 February, 1979

It has been minus 30 for a week. I don't care for this cold and its attendant problems. I spend a fortune in time gathering wood and recovering from the effort.

I went to Andy and Ruthie Runyan's house for dinner on 30 January. I caught my first lake trout there with my bare hands when it came off Runyan's hook and made a dash back over the ice into the hole through which Andy had just pulled it. I won the race and flipped it up onto the ice again out of the water.

We had a fine feed of moose, taters, carrots, and all the fixin's. This was my first taste of Ruthie Runyan's fine cooking. She has been a cook in numerous roadhouses all over central Alaska, and is quite well-known for her culinary expertise.

Yesternight I carved myself a smoking pipe out of birch, the wood that has heated me most of the winter. I left the saw-cut rough on the bottom, it being also a reminder of my efforts with the Swedesub saw all winter. On the front I have carved "Lake Louise, Alaska, 2/'79 RMO." It will forever remind me of my first winter in the Alaskan bush.

The "joy" of authorship. That's me writing this book on my old Royal manual typewriter. I'm smoking the pipe I carved out of birch, which is the wood that did most of the heating for me.

Wednesday, 14 February . . . A rough day's log

Thirty-eight below at 9:00 A.M. I asked Jan Hansen when it is supposed to get warm and she said, "Two weeks ago!" One gets very weary of this daily struggle against the elements, the need to gather wood, the need to keep a hot fire going all day and night, and the need to haul water.

11:15 A.M. The wind has seen fit to blow like a bastard again. I am extremely low on wood and water and feel as much like going for them as I feel like defecating in my boots and having them for lunch.

2:10 P.M. Wind is still blowing like the clappers right past my door. Impossible to cut wood out there. I made three cuts and froze my right hand all to hell. Must get wood. Should get water. Dishes and general dirt piling up. Hope the wine holds out till the end of this winter!

6:50 P.M. This is Valentine's Day. What a sweetheart of a day! Wind is still blowing lickety-split. My evening's wood lies in ruins of long logs all over my floor waiting to be cut up, because it is impossible to work outside the door.

7:45 P.M. Wood all cut up and stacked, floor somewhat clean. Wind still going strong, a good 20 mph gusting to 30 plus. Temp is steady at 20 below zero. It is a cold dark night. Very bleak outside.

This weather really taxes me. You can get sort of used to it and can function pretty well, but that does not mean you like it.

8:20 P.M. The snow on the lake is whipped into waves and pockmarks like a shallow lake in a stiff summer breeze, then quick-frozen. Wind still blowing. Time for me to eat. Meat and potatoes tonight.

10:30 P.M. Wind still blows hard as I sit to have what amounts to a fantastic dinner: beef chunks, potatoes, gravy, and the last of my butter; also a little onion for the meat, and some wine.

11:55 P.M. Just rounding onto midnight. Wind still blowing hard, temp is minus 22 degrees F. Cold enough, but moderated by a good meal.

Thursday morning, 15 February

Twenty below, nearly dead calm. Wind quit between four and six A.M.

(Close of a rough day's log.)

[*That cold spell lasted three weeks. My spirits waxed with each hope of warmer weather and waned as each new day brought nothing but more and more cold. For three straight weeks it was never warmer than 20 below zero; most of the time not warmer than 30 below.*]

Friday, 16 February

Caribou! At least six on the lake. Golden in the sunlight, they trotted into the cover of the trees as I watched.

Tuesday, 6 March

First notes in three weeks. February finally wound down and with it went the worst of the cold weather. I feel listless and want to do nothing. I guess I used up a lot of energy last month.

Fifteen above feels really warm!

Saturday, 10 March

Temp now 25 above, highest since last November. Today I cleaned my cabin. At least I now feel like doing something with myself instead of just reading and sleeping. I have to haul wood only about every other day now, and I just let the fire go out overnight. During the whole of last month I was burning wood at the rate of a cord every ten days.

Sunday, 11 March

From my Alaskan adventure so far I have learned that I get along very well with a wilderness environment (except the long and dark cold!) and all the critters in it. The moose, rabbits, ptarmigan, owls, foxes, weasels, etc., all come right up to the cabin with no apparent fear. I have come to resent the presence of inconsiderate humans, especially unobservant noisy louts like the two fellows who got within 25 yards of a moose, then shouted to one another about fresh moose tracks, and wondered where in hell was the moose. They never saw the moose. I watched this whole fiasco from my cabin high on the hill above them.

Sunday, 8 April

As I rise and greet my frozen cabin with a curse, the first thing I do after lighting the stove is have a glass of ice water to warm me up.

Every morn these last two weeks I've got up, lit the fire, then got myself outside as fast as I could to drink my coffee. I can't stand to be inside the damp dark cabin where I was confined during the long winter.

Thursday, 12 April

Five thirty A.M. and 5 degrees outside. Very cold in the cabin. This is a %&$%#@ waste of time! I can't sleep and need to, so I lay in bed ten or twelve hours until the rising sun starts to warm up the cabin. Then I have to build a fire and burn a ton of wood to get the cabin warm. Then I run out of wood, so I have to go get some more from my spot on the hillside 300 yards away. By the time I'm warm, awake, and have enough wood to last all day (with some left over for the next morning) I'm all tired out or it is dark and I may as well go to bed. Damn this cold!

This morning when I opened the barrel stove to build a fire a ton of ashes fell out onto the floor. I lost my temper and thrashed a trough in the ashes to get some more room in the stove, thus spilling more ashes onto myself and the floor. I cussed and coughed for an hour and am still doing so. (I wanted lots of ashes inside the stove to raise the fire level up nearer the top of the stove in order to make better use of the stovetop for cooking.)

I find that seven months of extremely cold weather tends to wear down my spirit excessively. No more Alaskan winters, thank you. I wonder if I'd feel this way if I didn't have the drudgery and discomfort of hauling wood every day and freezing every night.

Wednesday, 18 April

As one spends time in such a place, where his hours are his and his alone, shared only with those of the near wild creatures, one finds that he picks up some of the natural habits of these creatures. Twice now I have been able to observe my reaction on encountering "myself" in the woods unexpectedly. In both instances I had removed my coat and hat as I warmed to my daily chore of gathering fuel, and I had left them hanging on a tree in my hillside woodlot. I carried a load of wood up the hill to the cabin and passed some time at the cabin for one reason or another, and by the time I returned to the hillside I had quite forgotten I had left said hat and coat hanging on a limb like a scarecrow. When I came on the "person" standing on my hillside, I was at once outraged and scared, inclined to run away before I was seen by the "intruder."

It is no wonder, then, that I hate the intrusion of any outsiders, meaning other people, who come by the cabin unannounced or unexpected, simply skiing or walking by. I feel what any moose, squirrel, fox, caribou, or whatever, must surely feel: Someone who does not belong here is interfering with the peace and quiet of the neighborhood.

Sunday, 22 April

Today I went to get some wood only to discover the ground is bare and there is enough wood lying on the ground, visible through the melted snow, to get me through the summer. What a relief! For the past three days every time the sun came out and the temperature remained reasonable throughout the day, I found myself wanting to take a nap at midday. Now I realize this was the reaction to finally being able to let my guard down after the long winter. I finally realized I didn't have to brace myself against the cold all day and night.

Spring finally arrived and with it the author got outside as often as possible to soak up the sun and take a much-needed, and hard-won, rest.

Today I reminisced about the past winter. I remembered huddling near my stove last February, burning the last few scraps of wood, hoping it would warm up outside. I didn't want to go outside for any reason, yet I knew that if I didn't, I would freeze. I usually sat by the stove until the sun started down. Then I knew I had to go get the wood, tired and weak and usually hungry as I was, for I knew that although it was 30 below zero outside, I had fourteen hours of darkness ahead of me during which it would only get colder. Out I would go to find a dead standing tree, anything decent from about four inches up to the biggest, which were about nine inches' diameter. I'd knock it down with my Swede saw (I never used a chain saw . . . I could not afford the gas for one even if someone had given me a chain saw), cut that tree into ten-foot sections that I could pack to the cabin on my shoulder, carry them to the cabin, and cut them to a length that would fit into the barrel stove. I did exactly no wood splitting, because it was not necessary.

Once I had my night's wood in, I would come inside to fix something for dinner. Dinner would be anything filling that didn't take too much time or energy to cook. I ate a lot of beans, stew, rice, things like that. Vast volumes of bacon grease. Honey by the cup.

I would then read by kerosene lamp, seeking some kind of escape from my surroundings, until I could no longer tolerate sitting in my chair. Then I'd lie on the bed and continue to read, always getting as close to the lamp as I could . . . never close enough! When cold and fatigue overcame me I would get under all the covers I had and sleep fitfully for ten or twelve hours. Every two or three hours during the night I would have to get up to re-stoke the fire. No matter how diligently I stoked that fire all night, each morning would find the water in my reservoir and in my pitcher frozen.

I would arise in the morning with my usual curse, dress with all my outdoor duds, coat, hat, gloves and all, build the fire up and huddle next to it for a couple of hours as the room and everything in it slowly thawed. Then I would gradually remove my coat and other heavy clothing and settle down by my fire to read until the swiftly setting sun roused me to do it all over again.

So it's no wonder I am having reactions to the warming weather, now that it's slowly getting reasonable outside. I think it'll be a long time indeed until I can again look forward to cold weather and snow.

And so ends my journal excerpt.

With the gradual coming of spring and more carefree weather, my mood gradually improved. I spent the summer working for one of the lodges at the lake. As summer went along it dawned gradually on me I didn't want to leave Alaska for the coming winter, as I had sworn I would. In fact, I found to my utter amazement I was actually looking forward to it! I don't know why this happened. I did have the offer of a room for the winter at the lodge, but that offer did not pan out, and I spent the majority of my second winter in my little cabin at Army Point. I was able to enjoy the second winter quite a lot, since I knew I had already been through the worst Alaska had to offer. But there were other reasons that made winter number two easier.

That second winter I had the use of a snowmobile, which was very kindly loaned to me by JoAn and Whitey Moore. They had just bought a cabin on the lake. I spent part of my second winter running a very modest trapline on their snowmachine, learning how trapping is supposed to be done. I hauled wood with the snowmachine and also burned oil while I was gone tending my trapline, so I didn't have the awful burden of daily woodcutting that I had the first winter. The loan of that snowmobile made the biggest difference in my mood, as it let me get out and about and do something besides sit on my duff in misery.

Running the trapline gave me something to do. The trapping occupied my mind and very greatly shortened the winter. During my third winter I ran a serious trapline of about 80–100 miles. Winter number three absolutely flew by, and it was spring far too soon for the ardent trapper!

I think there was another reason I didn't want to go back to the lower forty-eight for my second Alaskan winter. I had come to realize how foolish and artificial are so many of the things and ideas found in polite society. These unnecessary items and ideas of "civilization" had annoyed me for a long time while I was a part of it, things like noisy music, traffic, stink of pollution, endlessly barking dogs, etc. My self-imposed winter's isolation gave clarity to my opinions as to how much or how little of the trappings of "society" I found really necessary. Why should I go back to where I don't belong?

Here's one last journal note:

Friday, 11 May

Time cards and schedules and "tea at four" and computers and hamburger stands all do not belong here in the wilderness. There is no need to know what time it is to know if you're hungry. No need to go to bed at a certain hour, no lunch whistle, no "payments." No need for any of the trappings of lunacy called civilization.

I have decided to make Alaska my home for the foreseeable future. I enjoy and love Alaska so much that I would be a fool indeed to leave all this for anything the lower forty-eight has to offer. I enjoy this country too much to leave Alaska behind for polluted air and traffic jams.

Amen. I like Alaska. Maybe you will too. But then, Alaska is not for everyone.

The Call of Wild Country

T he previous portion of this book and my Army Point journal notes were all about my first winter in Alaska. I came to realize the plans I had made, which took me to Alaska in the first place, had not really been fulfilled. I had spent an interesting winter in my cabin on Army Point, but had not done a tenth of the things I had set out to do when I left Denver. While I gained tremendous insight in how to live while truly roughing it I had never intended to spend all my time hauling wood and shivering. I wanted to explore, walk in the woods, enjoy Alaska, and get the feeling of having accomplished something with my time. I had especially planned to spend lots of time in Alaska learning a great deal more about firearms than I knew when I left Denver. My research into the world of firearms was something I knew I'd need for the rest of my life, and I had done essentially none of it. In short, I needed more time in the bush. My story of the Alaskan wilderness was not done, nor would it be for more than another decade. In all, I spent fourteen years in Alaska. Of them, nine years were in Anchorage and five in wild country. Of my years in the bush, the first three were spent at Lake Louise. My last years in Alaska were in the wilderness at a little red cabin near Lake Louise, and that's when things got really good. I learned at firsthand how comfortable one can be, and with that comfort came great accomplishments and great rewards. My final Alaskan years were some of the best times of my life in many ways, and when I learned a great deal about my chosen profession.

What happens to a person who has a great craving, or need, for wild county, spends five years living in it, and then moves to the city? Does the craving go away, or get stronger? What about the things learned in the woods that seep into one's consciousness? Do they persist, or are they lost? What insight into the world does one gain from such unusual activity? Do the tricks, the skills, the knowledge, the cravings, and all the other feelings go away? Perhaps the biggest question: Can one remain in the city or in close proximity to other people after such exposure to life in the bush? The simple answer: No, one can't.

One of the things that persisted for me is the great love for silence I acquired in the bush. Some folks have to have the hustle and bustle of the city and would be happiest in the middle of New York. I am the opposite. I've been to New York and hope never to be there again. Out in the woods or backcountry there is none of the banging and grinding of the city. Instead there's the sound of the wind in the trees, the rush of running water near a stream, the occasional call of a bird or barking chatter of a squirrel, but for the most part what you get is peaceful silence. I like that. The noise and bustle of the city are not what I wanted after my time in bush Alaska, though I had to endure some of that to get where I am today.

It might well be asked: What drove me to go to Alaska in the first place? The answer to that is not simple. There was no pending apocalypse. No acts of government-inspired terror had driven me away from Colorado into the northern wilds. Perhaps the simplest answer is that I was at my wit's end as to what to do with myself. I had been laid off from a lucrative job at Martin Marietta, working on the Viking Mars Lander. I had turned my efforts to gunsmithing, setting up an independent shop in the back of a gun store that catered to cops. I also did instruction and photography for the

John Robert Powers Modeling Agency. After Viking I lived in the basement of my friend Curt Lund's house on the southern skirts of Denver. Curt was also a shooter, and we had many good times and a lot of competition together. I had known him for several years, and one of the matches in which we competed led me to becoming a gun writer. Because of intervening work with the Viking project my gun writing halted for a few years. But once I got laid off, I thought it was a good idea to get back into it.

In my basement apartment I pushed myself hard as a gun writer. I had some good publishing success in some tough markets, like *The American Rifleman*, under my belt. My gun-writing work went on for about two years there. But Curt, my landlord, was about to get married, and really didn't want me living in his basement. I could understand that, but where could I go? What could I do? By then I was becoming fairly well established in the gun-reportage press, but I felt I didn't know as much as I ought to about my gun work. I wanted to go somewhere away from town, to set up a sort of testing facility where I could study guns, get to really become an expert on all aspects of them, and then I figured I'd be able to sell my writing a lot easier, and to more markets. I needed a place where no one would interfere with me and the rent was zero.

My life in Denver had taken me to New Mexico for the Viking job, and thankfully I had not accumulated all the, er, crap that I now possess. I was mobile out of necessity. I had long wondered about both Africa and Alaska. Ever since I was a kid, reading John Taylor's *Pondoro* and *African Rifles and Cartridges*, I had wanted to go to Africa. I wanted to become a bona fide big-game hunter. I had an elephant rifle, my Churchill double 470, but didn't know anyone in Africa. Also, I could not drive to Africa. So when it was time to leave Denver, by reluctant default I went to Alaska.

Of course I had no idea what Alaska was like, but I knew there was lots of open, wild country there, and all that wide-open wilderness appealed to me as being a fine and easy place to live. (Boy, was I stupid!) So when it came time to move out of my basement digs I decided to move to Alaska to find my place there, and embark on a solid test regiment of all sorts of firearms. In fact I had no other place to go. No one I knew was hiring technicians for the kind of critical and highly skilled work I had done on Viking. The folks with whom I had worked at White Sands in New Mexico didn't need anyone. More's the pity because there was a girl named Vicki in Las Cruces with whom I really wanted to spend more time, but had to abandon that idea . . . as it turned out, forever. So I followed my trail to Alaska on the ongoing path of the adventurer. As I noted in the beginning of this book I bit off nearly more than I could chew, that first winter. As it worked out, I did not do any serious gun testing during my three years at Army Point, but did learn a little about what Alaskans were doing with their guns.

For the three summers after my first Alaskan winter in that uninsulated cabin at Army Point I had good jobs. The first summer I worked for one of the local lodges. The next summer I was with the new lodge owners as a fishing guide, taking clients down the Gulkana river, and finally I spent a summer working for the State Fish & Wildlife Protection Division as a summertime law enforcement aide on Kodiak and Afognak islands. During my second winter I trapped, and the third winter trapped with a vengeance. All of this adventuring gave me insight into people and the outdoors, but not much into the realm of firearms, and it wasn't making me rich. I knew I needed to do something different, something better. Then, in the fall, just before the beginning of my fourth Alaskan year, I sold a piece of property I owned in Colorado, up in South Park near Quartzville. With money in the bank I moved 200 miles to Anchorage, got an apartment, updated my photo gear, and set myself up as a commercial freelance photographer. That went well, but again I did zero gun testing. I don't believe I fired a shot in close to nine years. Some years later, oil prices—on which much of the Anchorage economy depended—dropped drastically and I again found myself out of both funds and ideas. And so I went back to my beloved wilderness and finally got some things done. Here's a brief look at my life in Anchorage, how I got back to my beloved wild country, and what wonderful, truly incredible, things happened to me there.

Photography in Anchorage

Despite my three years of absorbing the wild life in wild country and making it part of my rough-cut inner makeup, and despite my well-entrenched preference for the simple things in life, I at least had the intelligence to wear a coat and tie when I called on prospective big-dollar clients to offer them my photo services. This included Sohio Alaska Petroleum Company, which became one of my more regular and lucrative clients. My fellow freelancers could not understand why I got the big-oil business they coveted, yet they refused to look in the mirror to see what a shabby picture they presented to these clients. Sohio does not hire bums, nor anyone who looks like one, to work for them, and those guys just didn't get it. That was to me both mighty humorous and extremely satisfying.

There was another factor in my getting those jobs. My first contact at Sohio was a fellow named Frank Baker. On showing him my photo portfolio I happened to mention guns, or there may have been some photos from my gun writing in the portfolio. As luck had it, Frank was an avid shooter and outdoorsman. He and I talked about guns for a long time in his office on our first meeting, and then it was time for me to leave. I had become used to rejections by other clients in town, and expected the same from Frank. As I was leaving

I asked him to keep me in mind if he had a need for my services as a photographer. I well recall his words: "Oh, we'll use you."

And use me he did! Time after time, year after year, Frank put me to some very hard work. I became good friends with many of the Sohio personnel, got to know most of the top dogs in the oil business—and quite a few politicians—on a first-name basis, and made out quite well, mostly because I knew enough to wear a tie to my interview, and had the good luck to talk guns with the guy who did the hiring. Frank and I went hiking, hunting, and cross-country skiing together, and became quite good friends. I think he felt guilty about using me all the time, but hey, I delivered the goods.

Frank Baker, my contact at Sohio, became a good friend. We skied, hiked, and hunted together.

I had little trouble fitting into society, which somewhat surprised me. I started dating a girl I met on one of my Sohio assignments. She was a good deal younger than I, and I've always looked young for my age—though my time on the trapline definitely aged me—so she and I got along well enough. My work for Sohio required me to take publicity photos, usually of what's commonly called grip-and-grins, of the company head giving away money. The donor and recipient shake hands (the grip) and smile for the camera (the grin). One of my first jobs for Sohio was to cover an event where some palooka was giving some money to the Boys and Girls' Club of Anchorage. I went, and got a big surprise at the size of the check. It was for $50,000. I got the grip-and-grin, but wanted more, so I grabbed the palooka who gave away the money, dragged him down the hall away from the main event, and got him to sit in the middle of a bunch of the boys and girls who were the objects of the cash donation. I made him wave at the camera from the middle of that group. I ordered him around and generally treated him like some yokel I had grabbed off the street. I told him what to do and how to do it. I got my photo of the palooka looking like just another one of the kids to which he had just donated a big pile of money. My photo turned out to be a big hit with the company and, as it turned out, with the palooka himself. I was later surprised to find out my "palooka" was in fact George Nelson, CEO of Sohio Alaska Petroleum Company and one of the biggest of the bigwigs in the oil industry in Alaska. He and I became friends over the succeeding years. (He, too, had a young girl-friend.) Through my photo work I also got to know the governor, city mayor, and quite a few other bigwigs in town on a first-name basis. I got Christmas cards from Governor Sheffield, in fact.

Once I had my photos of events like that money-giveaway I had to go home and process the black & white film, dry it, edit the shots, and make 8x10 prints, all that same night. Then I'd deliver the stack of prints to the security guys at the Sohio building, usually around two or three in the morning. Then it was back home to bed. As often as not the phone would wake me the next morning with another assignment. I developed the ability to sound wide awake on the phone even if it was only thirty seconds after I had been awakened. The caller was usually Frank Baker, my contact at Sohio, with another assignment or two. I suspect my being extremely fit permitted me to do that kind of work for quite a few years, and I was by no means a young man at the time. Today it takes several hours for me to even begin to sound reasonably awake after I open my eyes in the morning. Chalk that working success up to my outdoor living at Lake Louise. However, I intend never to step into a darkroom again during the remainder of my life.

Things went quite well in Anchorage for about nine years. During that time I became fairly well known as a photographer around that town. Many people would give me a friendly greeting as I went around town, though I confess I had no idea who most of them were. I had a lovely girlfriend, decent work from a variety of important clients, became a "shooter" (staff photographer) for the *Anchorage Times* newspaper, and even got my art photos in the permanent collection of the University of Alaska. I had long been a fan of Ansel Adams, and most of my art photos are of Alaskan wilderness in one form or another. A few of them are in this book.

Afognak Beach

Old Shack on Stream

Birch & Pond

Nabesna Road

I also took a job as staff photographer and, as it happened, computer guru, for Pacific Quest Publishing, which did *Alaska Flying*
magazine, several other Alaska-related magazines, and the beautiful but short-lived *Outpost* in-flight magazine. My work for various clients took me by air all over Alaska. I flew to Deadhorse on
the Sohio 727 jet and spent some time in its cockpit, even during landing. On the way back from Deadhorse we circled Mount
McKinley and I got some exclusive photos of it from the air. I flew
to the western end of Alaska to Ruby and Emmonak and other
tiny villages on assignment. Out there I flew with the late, great
Ellen Paneok, Native bush pilot, author, artist, commercial and
stunt pilot. I got to watch from the front seat as she landed on what
looked like a driveway partially blocked with oil barrels, but was in
fact the runway of an airport serving a tiny village. I also got close
to the very end, the southernmost point, of the Aleutian Chain on
a Sohio assignment. I saw more of Alaska than most people ever do,
so I guess I can say my stint at commercial photography was one of
the best jobs I've ever had.

I got ambitious and signed up for the largest-area studio in the city, right next to Merrill Field airport. But no sooner was my name on the rental contract then the price of oil went into the basement. Sohio had hired a full-time photographer during my sojourn at the *Anchorage Times*, so I was never even considered as a candidate for the job I had done for them as a freelancer for so many years. Once again I quickly found myself without any significant income (the eternal curse of the adventurer), and had to downsize. I gave up the studio and for a few months actually lived in my travel trailer with my beloved cat outside the offices of that publishing company. My good friend the photographer Danny Daniels had given me a cat he found on his doorstep with her ears frozen off. I took her in, named her Tiger, and kept her as long as I could. Living in my travel trailer didn't last long, so my cat and I moved just out of town to a low-priced apartment in Eagle River. Things didn't get better, so I decided it was time to give it all up and find something else to do.

About that time old friend Jack Hansen, who had owned Evergreen Lodge at Lake Louise, phoned me. He had a computer problem and knew I was clever with them. I fixed his problem, and as we chewed the fat afterward I told him I was at my wit's end as to what to do with myself. Jack had sold the lodge a few years before, and then got a divorce. The buyers of the lodge were also experiencing the crunch of low oil prices, and Jack was about to move back to the lake and resume ownership and control of the lodge. He thought he might need some help, so he invited me to come out to Lake Louise again and take an empty room in the lodge. At that time, the call of the wild was starting to make its presence known again. I was getting fed up with city life and all it held—or didn't hold—for me. Here was a chance to move back to Lake Louise! Well, why not? So Tiger and I moved into Jack's lodge.

Things were not great living in the same dwelling with Jack. Tiger was sick, getting sicker all the time, and Jack did not like cats. My room was above a generator shed and the exhaust gas leaked into the room. This did neither me nor my cat any good. Finally

I could take it no longer and got in touch with Don MacArthur, who owned a little rental cabin on the long road to his house. I was able to rent the cabin, which at the time was painted red. Tiger and I went to look the rental cabin over. My kitty looked around at the place and didn't like it. She wanted out of it. It was like she was telling me, "Ray, I won't be here with you." She had seen the future. I arranged to move in there, but just before I did so, my cat's illness got much worse (she had come to me infected with feline leukemia) and I took her to Anchorage to a vet. He told me there was nothing he could do for her. And so I lost my beloved best friend just as I moved into Red Cabin.

Tiger, my precious cat, came to me with her ears frozen off. She had to leave early, and never lived at Red Cabin. That built-in trap box was handy.

Red Cabin

To get to Red Cabin you drove to the very end of the Lake Louise road. The road ended in a causeway of constantly flowing water, deep but not very wide, and it was open water year around. To cross the causeway you could use a small boat that was chained there (winter or summer), or if you were brave, in winter you could drive a big circle around the causeway's open water on the lake ice. Generally no one did that. MacArthur had vehicles on both sides of this causeway so he could come and go at his wish. This causeway was a narrow gap between tiny Dinty Lake to the south and big Lake Louise to the north. Water always flowed through between them, which kept the causeway open. Once across the causeway there was well over a mile of rough road leading to another water crossing, shallow this time, but very wide, maybe forty yards. This was a river that flowed out of Little Lake Louise, past Red Cabin, and eventually into big Lake Louise. If you knew your way and were brave, you could drive across this second waterway (4WD recommended). Once across that, you turned sharply to the left and followed the road parallel with the river about another quarter mile to Red Cabin. The road continued past the cabin deeper into the woods to the MacArthur residence, which was about another mile past Red Cabin. As it turned out, I was able to drive my Land Cruiser through the deep, narrow water of the causeway, even though the water came briefly over my hood. Any spectators there always dropped their jaws when I drove through the causeway. Of course the second, wider but shallower, crossing held no terrors for me or my Land Cruiser.

Here's what the river-side of Red Cabin looked like. This south-facing side got good sun. The ground dropped steeply to the river, which was about fifty yards south of the back porch, behind the camera.

The cabin consisted of three rooms, bedroom, main room with kitchen, and a second cubby that could have been another bedroom, but which served as my reloading room. The cabin had an arctic entry, which is a small room between the main room and the outdoors, with inner and outer doors. That is a must on a wilderness cabin, by the way. The main door was on the north side and faced the road and a small parking area where I kept the car. The road was private, on private land, serving only myself and the landlord, Don MacArthur. So the cabin saw only the occasional traffic of the MacArthur family going to or from town, and whoever came to visit them. The south side of Red Cabin faced the river, which was down a slope about fifty yards away. The cabin had a porch facing the river. Some evergreens bordered the porch closely. A path led from the cabin to a small dock jutting into the river, and that's where I got my drinking water. I'd go to the far end of the dock to dip my water buckets into the river for my drinking supply. Again, as when I lived on Army Point nearly a decade earlier, I did exactly no boiling of the water before drinking it.

This is the view to the southwest from the porch of Red Cabin. The tree line touching the sky is Cookie's Ridge. Over it to the southeast are Cookie's and Ray's Lakes. The barren area in the lower center is the frozen river.

Red Cabin had propane lights and a propane cooking stove, and heat was by a good oil-burning stove. Don had installed a small solar panel on the roof that fed a car battery. Connected to that was an old car radio, which worked well. There was no woodstove, which meant I didn't have to scrounge firewood. If it had been my cabin I would have provided an alternate means of heating with some sort of wood-burning stove at hand, if for some reason it became impossible to get fuel oil. Compared to the rough cabin I had lived in the better part of three years on Army Point, this was a dream. It had good insulation everywhere. It was the sort of dwelling I had always wanted, especially after I realized and had endured the grand limitations of my cabin on Army Point. The comfort and setup of Red Cabin was what I had imagined before I left the lower forty-eight to come north. I had been working toward such a cabin during my time in Anchorage. I had tried to save enough money to buy a piece of land in the bush and build a small house. It would have been much like Red Cabin, though smaller. I had never been able to save enough money, so I ended up renting.

I'm sitting on the west wall of the main room of Red Cabin, this before I painted the walls white. I'm checkering a handgun grip panel. This was a far more comfortable situation than my Army Point cabin of a decade earlier. The door to the right leads to the bedroom.

This is the same main room looking north, toward the road outside. The door at the left, beyond the water storage tank, leads to the arctic entry.

Down a step to the east and you're in my reloading room. I learned a lot here, and it all paid off.

Although it took a while for me to realize it, it was a joy to be back in the woods, away from the bustle and madness that I had experienced in Anchorage, and to some extent at Evergreen Lodge. Here, my time was mine. I didn't have to share a dwelling with anyone, and didn't have any chores other than attempting, the best way I could, to provide for myself.

I moved all my plunder into the cabin as quickly as I could get out of Evergreen Lodge. I didn't own a lot of stuff, but had lots of guns and reloading supplies. As I grew more at peace in Red Cabin I realized I could finally do what I had intended to do ever since I made plans to leave Denver, and that was to get heavily involved with testing, experimenting with, and studying the firearms that have always fascinated me, and which had provided me with much of my livelihood before I became a serious photographer. I was done with professional photography, and I think I knew it by the time I left Anchorage for good. Of course I'd need to take photos of the various guns I intended to study and write about, but I didn't consider that to be quite the same. As for commercial photography, I'd been there, done that, and had become quite sick and tired of it. I was determined to get back into gun writing with a passion. It had been a viable source of income for me in long years past, and the subject held considerable interest for me, but I had lost contact with my previous editors. I had no particular magazine or book in mind, but I still had one or two friends in the publishing business. One of these was Ken Warner, my first editor when he was at the NRA's *The American Rifleman*. He turned out to be a big help in suggesting where I might sell my stories. Ken had become involved with DBI Books, which published *Gun Digest* and a host of other outdoor, gun-related books, and I did some writing for them. I also eventually did quite a bit of writing for several Australian gun magazines. But first I had to deal with my biggest problem, the loss of my beloved cat.

As might be expected I was heartsick for a long time. I took to walking in the woods as much as I was able, to ease the pain of my loss. It was early spring, and deep snow was everywhere. It may not seem a big thing to you, dear reader, that I get so attached to my "kids." But that is how I am. My friend Danny Daniels was one of the very few who understood what that cat meant to me. He stood by me in my grief, and that helped me a lot. So my time at Red Cabin began in great sorrow, which continued in earnest for several weeks.

As I walked through the woods in my solitude I had noticed that I often felt as if I were being watched. At first, I gave this feeling no second thought, but the feeling kept popping up. It was not always there, but on certain occasions I felt it strongly. It was like the old trick of staring at the back of someone's neck in a classroom or library to make them turn around. That's what this felt like, amplified. One day I decided to see if someone was actually watching me. The next time I experienced this feeling I looked around carefully and finally saw a squirrel behind a branch, one eye showing, watching and waiting for me to go away so he could get on with his business. I began to pay more attention. After a short while, whenever I felt I was being watched I always found someone, a bird or a squirrel, sometimes an owl, glaring at me, deep in their territory. I wondered long and hard about that. Imagine you have spent your entire life in the woods, paying attention to these feelings, which I'm sure every bright-eyed critter out there must have. If I, a mere human, city bred and raised, could develop such a sense, how much stronger must it be in, say, a fox or in a squirrel. To that, add their far-better hearing and sense of smell, and one gets a picture that the silent wilderness must be an extremely active and interesting place for all the animals that call it home.

I'm somewhat disappointed that I no longer get that feeling. Too much time in the city? My current home is in pretty wild country, far away from any city. The largest town—a small one—is thirty miles away. My closest neighbor is a quarter-mile away. There are a few red squirrels around here, but they seem to pay me little attention. Maybe the squirrels and birds are so used to seeing me they no longer consider it a breach of their space, and after a glance they just ignore me. However, I am very much aware of when one of my cats stares at me, even if I can't see him. In fact I find it impossible to concentrate when that's happening. But I think that's a special situation. I used to have upward of fifteen cats here, mostly wild but dependent on me for food. Yet when I went on a walk, I never saw a cat, and never felt any of them watching me. So my best guess is my hard-won sensitivity is no longer with me.

Along similar lines, I mentioned the ptarmigan would commonly play near my cabin, but if I were going out hunting they would all disappear from view. Somehow, they knew what I was up to. I believe they had the capacity to read my mind, or at least understand my intent. My cats today show a strong sense of knowing my mood, even if I have not said a word, or even moved. One of them, Homer, knows exactly when I am hungry, and he makes a beeline for me when I head for the refrigerator. He doesn't need to see or even hear me, he just knows what's in my mind. He knows very well how to home in on the food source, and that in fact is how he got his name.

I've had the ability most of my life to be able to relate to animals closely. I guess that began in my childhood. We always had a dog around the house. I had always been on good terms with the house dog throughout my youth, but didn't quite realize what effect I had been having on them until the events of one day in Ann Arbor. I was attending the University of Michigan there, forty miles north of our family home. One day our family dog, Tuffy, appeared on my front lawn in Ann Arbor. He had traveled up those forty miles—how, I'll never know, because he was an old dog at the time—to visit me at school. It was not too long after that he died, so I guess he came to say good-bye. I was moved by his visitation. I had no idea he thought that much of me, but it made a great impression on me. I had always been kind to the family pet, unlike other members of my family. My mother and I had soft spots for them, and I guess they knew it. Many times over the years when I visited the home of friends who had pets, they would remark that their normally distant cat or dog seemed to easily accept me. I always found it to be comforting when the one guaranteed-honest soul in the house took a liking to me. One early spring day at Red Cabin I visited Sherm and Peggy Reynolds in their fine log cabin across Little Lake Louise. I had recently met them but had never visited them before. These folks had a dog that really didn't like visitors. By then I was used to the effect I had on other folks' dogs, so I understood their surprise when their dog came to me all friendly. I think they were jealous. I just smiled. The Reynoldses ran Bush Landscaping & Nursery in Anchorage for about forty years and visited Little Lake Louise often. They became good friends all during my stay at Red Cabin.

I had a battered Ski-Doo Bombardier TNT snowmachine with an engine I had rebuilt. I built a trap box for the back of it, and used that machine to set out a few traps late in the season. I was not nearly as heavily involved in trapping as I had been a decade before. My heart was not in it. It no longer appealed to me, other than being something to do so I could get away from the lodge. One's close and frequent association with wild animals of all types makes one aware of their joys, their struggles, and all the activities of their lives, to the point where the person with at least a little intelligence comes to sympathize with them. The inevitable outcome of that feeling is that one becomes extremely reluctant to take any of their lives.

That, probably, is the biggest and most enduring outcome for me of my time spent in the Alaskan bush. Today I am fairly well known as one of the more respected professional testers of firearms, to the extent that major manufacturers have significantly altered their products in response to my published comments and suggestions. However, I no longer have any interest whatsoever in hunting. I don't kill anything, except those predators that threaten my domestic animals. And mosquitoes. It may be that the reader will think I'm soft in the head, and personally I don't care. Many of my human friends are hunters. Good for them, I say. But my personal experiences have made it clear to me there are other, better, options than killing and eating my friends. The life of the mouse is just as important to him as is the life of the elephant, or yours to you. I'd far rather rejoice in friendship with my animal friends than, like some two-fisted moron once said long ago, "Whack 'em and stack 'em." Thing is, you learn nothing about what really matters by blindly killing things. I learned that my wilderness friends were perfectly capable of reasoning, and that they could completely understand my words, thoughts, and intents. Does that make them beneath humans? Hardly. Compared to the average woods-dwelling animal, we are deaf, blind, clumsy, arrogant, rough, insensitive, and just plain stupid. When I look into the eyes of a wild creature I see a spark of intelligence instead of the all-too-common blank wall of stupidity one sees in so many human faces. Don't believe me? Try it. Of course, you can't, because it takes years of living in close proximity to them before you can come to understand what you're seeing, if you can in fact get close enough to see into their eyes and have them look honestly into yours. The average dog or cat isn't in the same league. I speak here of many years' ongoing evaluation, not the sort of thing one can pick up in an afternoon. In spite of all that, I confess I was not yet entirely done with hunting when I lived at Red Cabin.

So as I said, my heart was not in my trapping and I eventually quit it altogether. But just before I pulled all my traps, I had managed to nearly catch a fox in a marten set. As always, the tracks in the snow told the whole story. Mr. Fox had got his foot in a small trap, broke it free from the set, and took the small trap with him. Not liking to leave a wounded animal out there, I spent considerable time sitting out with a rifle in the bitter cold, close to where I had placed that marten set, in hopes of seeing the wounded fox and ultimately nabbing him. Instead, as things worked out, he nabbed me, heart and soul, forever.

Cookie and the Beeks

The wonders found in nature, both imposingly large and intricately small—from the vista of the Grand Canyon to a monarch butterfly in flight—have been shown to have the power to lift people beyond the mundane day-to-day experience of the world, to spark a heightened moment in which we find ourselves inspired and awestruck.

—Chuck Norris

He came into my life one cold evening, the Northern Lights dancing overhead, the whole world quiet and white. I was standing there on the frozen road, looking at the stars, heartbroken over the loss of my pet cat, and morosely pondering my future. He came down the snow-covered road from the east, and didn't see me until he was just a few feet away. He caught some slight movement from me, stopped, and looked directly into my eyes. At that moment both our lives changed, entirely for the better. Neither he nor I were the least bit startled. I greeted the little fellow with soft words, and it seemed like he was reading my mind, knowing my thoughts. He showed no fear, and I showed him no animosity. I felt at that moment I was supremely blessed, as I looked into his eyes in wonder. He apparently saw in my mind that I meant him no harm. He didn't run. He just stood there looking at me, and somehow we communicated. We stood there a while, and presently I thought I'd give him some of the food I'd stockpiled for my late cat. I suspected this little guy might just want some of it. I told him to wait a minute, went inside and put some canned cat food into a bowl for him, and put it outside on the ground. I left him alone and watched from the cabin to see if he'd eat it. He did. Would he come again? I sincerely hoped so.

At the time, spring was slowly on its way, as always with great reluctance. I noted it in my Red Cabin Journal:

> And the sun shines and the wind blows and the clouds stream by, pausing only briefly to block the sun, a blushing maiden with a need to momentarily hide her smile. The birds patter on the porch, and the trees watch and wave outside my window. A sough of wind spins around my stovepipe, telling a tale as old as time and as inscrutable as the meaning of a moonbeam. Icicles deliver their drops to the ground with intravenous regularity. Spring is almost here, hiding just over the hills to the south.

Over the next few days my little fox friend came back to Red Cabin just about every evening for a handout. In short order he ate up all the cat food I had stored for my departed kitty. I looked forward to his visit every evening, about suppertime, and always found something for him to eat. Our newfound friendship seemed to mean as much to him as it did to me. His presence did a lot to take my mind off the pain of my recent loss. I realize it now but not at the time, that I was slowly letting my departed kitty go to her maker without holding on to her tail and trying to keep her with me. I had a living creature (with a much bigger tail!) right there in my yard to care for, feed, and worry about.

Cookie was a handsome rascal with a spark of intelligence in his eyes. He seemed to understand my every word and thought.

My new friend—he was a cross fox—had a wounded front foot, missing two toes. Clearly he had had that foot in a trap, and that trap had been set by me. He limped, and it took nearly a year for the limp to go away. He was not a young fellow, with gray on his muzzle and elsewhere. He looked healthy, and moved quite well. After a short time of feeding him, as I sat indoors, I would get a feeling, a hunch, that he was there outside, even though he usually came at different times of day. When I looked, having had that feeling, there he was. Over the months I came to *know* when he was there. It was no longer guesswork.

I used to sit with Cookie under the stars on mild nights, and we communicated mentally in a way that still gives me immense joy these many years later. He'd eat, taking food directly from my hand, and then go to his special spot on a little hill of snow, which gave him good visibility. Sometimes he'd jump up and look here or there, and suddenly depart. Usually some other critter like a moose or caribou would come into view after a minute or so. When they got close enough I could barely hear the slight noise they made, but the fox could hear them at probably five times the distance. The key point is he alerted me to their presence long before I was aware of it. That was to be mighty helpful later on.

THE BEEKS

I also had birds. Good grief, did I have birds! Within a few days of my moving into Red Cabin the gray jays (camp robbers) came for handouts and were not disappointed. Quickly they were able to eat out of my hand, and I got to know their individual faces and habits. I gave them all names, such as Buzzard, Bill, Gertelbeak, Flattop, Splittail, Peepkin, Little Sister, and others. There were two families, one that lived close to the cabin and the other from across the river to the southwest. They were rivals, and the closer family would chase the others off, but everyone got something to eat for as long as I lived at Red Cabin. A half dozen little chickadees would come for food. I gave all of them names too. They were Mr. and Mrs. Snowball, Sarge, Mini-Peep, Fuzzywings, Raggytail, and several others. I sent my mother a photo of one I called Snowflake. He was patient enough to pose for a picture sitting on my hand. Snowflake would fly in tight circles outside my window to get my attention, and give three sharp peeps pitched so high I could barely hear them.

There were also pine grosbeaks. These were stiff-feathered, very fast birds with short beaks. These guys fly through the woods like little rockets, twisting and dodging the trees like a fighter plane flying through a twisting canyon. They could hover, and generally hovered near my hand to take the birdseed I offered, usually sunflower seeds. One day, one of these guys (named Chicken) decided to land on my hand. While there, he demolished the whole pile of sunflower seeds. The hulls fell like rain. That's how I found out their feathers were quite stiff. The chickadees and gray jays were soft by comparison.

I also had a woodpecker as a regular customer. In my notes I identified him as either a hairy woodpecker or a three-toed, and then tried to come up with a name for him. My suggestions from the Red Cabin Journal listed "Needlebeak. Woody. Thunderpecker. (Good grief!) Whackerbeak. Peckerbeak. (Egad!) Thunderbeak."

I settled on Woody. One morning I went out onto the back porch to feed my birds. I heard a rustle in a tree next to the porch, but could not see who was making the rustling. I asked, "Who's there?" And heard "Tap-tap-tap!" on the tree trunk. I said, "Woody?" And I heard "Tap-tap-tap-tap-tap!" He knew his name. He had the ability to eat what the other birds could not, that which was frozen. I discovered he thought his food was apparently better for being beaten upon. He would stand next to fresh, soft, and still-warm food and bash the dickens out of some rock-hard morsel frozen to the porch rail.

There was a little mouse next to the house who, so far as I know, escaped the jaws of my little fox for as long as I lived there. I'd go to the mouse's front door and call him, and out he'd come, shyly, and get something to help him fight off the chill nights.

The pair of gray jays who first came to the cabin were named Buzzard and Bill. Buzzard, the female, was a most friendly soul. She was the first to follow me through the woods, and did that as long as I lived there. All along the trail she'd sing the prettiest tunes. Her mate was Bill, who was kind of grumpy. They had some kids that first summer. As they grew, the kids started coming to the cabin. One of them was highly entertaining. This fellow, whom I called the idiot son, later turned out to be one of the more intelligent birds. The first time he came, he took to attacking his reflection in the window. He'd charge it and use his beak and wings in a grand attempt to chase himself away. Often he'd wake me up in the morning, beating on the window, banging and tapping, pecking and flapping. Often he'd wake me when I didn't really want to be awakened. There were beak smudges all over my window. I called him Peepkin.

Peepkin often awakened me by beating on the window.

A red squirrel also came for handouts. I called him Rhodent after a character in long-ago (1959) *Dick Tracy*. He had the habit of gnawing on the back porch. I don't know why he wanted to eat the house, but that went on as long as I was there. The fox also never bothered him. I guess the cabin was out of bounds for eating your neighbors.

Not only were the birds entertaining and helpful, they also presented a challenge to me to identify the ones I couldn't name. As the weather got better, more and more varieties showed up. These were not only songbirds of a huge variety, but also ducks, trumpeter swans, eagles, gulls, and more. I attempted to identify them in various reference books. I'd make a sketch of the bird with my notes indicating the various color patches, then take that sketch to the reference books and see what it was. It sure as heck beat playing video games. From my journal:

Eight A.M., and the incredible bugling of a pair of trumpeter swans fills the morning air, echoing up and down the river valley. It's hard to believe this sound comes from a bird. Suddenly their calls take on a new strident urgency, and then comes the *ba-bama-bama-bama* of four large wings beating in unison hard against the icy water of the morning river. Quickly the pair of swans lifts off, airborne. The two giant black-headed white birds come racing up the river, side by side in perfect formation, wings synchronized, black beaks outstretched on their impossibly long necks, traveling close to forty miles an hour. They streak past the cabin at great speed toward the west, and the early morning sun turns them to gold.

Summer "Chores"

$\mathbf{M}$y time at the Red Cabin was some of the happiest and most productive of my life. Instead of cutting and hauling wood all day every day, like I had done at Army Point a decade earlier, I'd get out and walk around, hike the hills and see what was there, get the lay of the land, and enjoy myself outside. I had wilderness to explore, and I had wild animal and bird friends who walked and flew with me through the wilderness. From my journal:

> Took a walk in the woods today in a big loop. I started down toward the crossing and came back from the other direction. Buzzard the bird was with me most of the way. She is sure a delight. She sits on my rifle barrel, on the stock, on my shoulder, and on my hat all along the way. She gets a little treat now and then to keep her happy . . . I live for my time in the woods. I love being out with rifle in hand and sixgun at my belt. This is wonderful.

During my time there I had enough money (barely) to buy bullets, primers, and powder and—once in a while—food, and devoted myself to outdoor activities and a lot of gun testing. I was finally able to do some serious experimenting with my collection of handguns, rifles, and shotguns. I built a shooting bench. I had acquired a powerful and accurate air rifle, an RWS Diana Model 48. I put over 2,000 pellets through it at Red Cabin learning how to shoot offhand, and that practice has served me well all my life. I got some guff from ownership of it, though, largely because of my pronounced affinity for great big rifles. Andy Runyan asked me one day, "Ray, you've got a 458 and a 470. How'd you end up with a BB gun?"

I have long prided myself in my ability to put a fine oil finish onto a gun stock. I had time to examine my rifles and decided to redo most of them. One was a Savage-Anschutz 22 target rifle that I never could get to shoot. One of the photos in this book is of me on the back porch of Red Cabin, refinishing the rifle's fine birch stock prior to glass bedding it. Sadly, all it did was make an inaccurate rifle look good. I could never get that rifle to shoot as it should have, and eventually sold it off. Along with several other rifles and my two shotguns I also decided to refinish my Churchill double 470. In this book is a photo of me grinding away at the butt stock with sandpaper, hard at work on a $40,000 rifle. (Don't try that at home!) I refinished half a dozen rifles and several handgun grips, and as I did them I tried desperately to come up with a succinct description of my process of putting a fine oil finish onto a fine gun stock. I wrote many pages and took many photos, but ended up never publishing anything about it. The bottom line is I kept working on a stock with various techniques and substances until I got what I wanted. I could not satisfactorily describe the process.

Here I'm smoothing the birch stock of the Savage-Anschutz 22 target rifle prior to giving it an oil finish. Note my vest, a common comfort in Alaskan weather.

One of the rifles I did a whole lot of work on was my 458. When I got it the rifle had many things wrong with it. It didn't feed, sometime jammed completely, needed some new parts, had a clumsy, ugly stock, and other problems. It had, however, a heart of gold that remained for me to chisel out of it. I wrote forty pages of notes on that rifle at Red Cabin, and ultimately made it essentially perfect. It became my most useful rifle there. Along the way I learned enough about that cartridge that I became somewhat of an expert on the 458 Winchester Magnum. My friend Dr. Jasper I. Lillie of Michigan had sent me some Herter's bullets in two weights for it, and one of them, the 350 grain, developed into one of the best loads I've ever seen for the cartridge. I'll talk more about this rifle later, but briefly, I redid the whole thing, made it feed perfectly, reshaped the stock drastically, finished and checkered it—all at Red Cabin. I did some engraving on it there too, and that's a major part of this story.

Here I'm grinding off the old finish of my $40,000 Churchill 470 double rifle prior to refinishing and recheckering it. I engraved its gold nameplate with my initials.

My life that first summer at Red Cabin was full of activity. On a typical day I'd get up and eat something, then grab the 458 (it was light enough to carry and powerful enough to deal with the grizzlies who called that part of the world home), whistle for my gray jay friends, and take a hike through the woods. The gray jays would follow me, fluttering along from tree to tree, and when I took a rest there they'd be asking for a handout. If I had nothing to offer them they'd take it in stride, happy to just be along, having fun. I got to the point where I would pay close attention to their chatter, so I knew where they were, how many were there, and what sorts of things they talked about. Not literally, but I got a sense of their mood if I paid attention. They were telling me what there was to be seen. One day their chatter turned suddenly into calls of warning, loud strident cries that clearly meant danger. On their alarm I froze, looked around carefully, and through the brush spotted a lynx swimming the river. A short time later he walked out onto the road in front of me, just thirty-five yards away. Without the warning from my birds I would never have seen him. They also told me when caribou or moose were about.

I walked the surrounding hills and dales with a vengeance. I went a couple miles north, as far as an overlook to Larson Bay on Lake Louise. I had the use of a small rowboat, so I could cross the river and walk south, exploring. I went south several miles, far enough to get to some of the lakes I had explored and trapped a decade before. That might not sound like much distance, but the country around Lake Louise is largely muskeg interspersed with steep hills, which doesn't give you an easy walk by any means.

Then I'd come home and rustle some grub. I was largely broke, usually waiting for payment from Australia or from some U.S.-based magazines to which I had sold something, so my grub was not fancy. I did a lot of blueberry picking. In season I shot a duck or two. I didn't seem to have much luck fishing. I recall one day I found a few twenty-five cent pieces, so I was able to go to one of the lodges and buy a jar of beans, and that was a big treat. After my dinner I'd feed my birds and the fox if he was around. I always managed to find something for my little friends to eat.

The next day I might do some reading and writing, maybe take some photos, or maybe work on the snowmachine engine on the kitchen table. Often I'd do some bullet casting or other reloading chores, or take one or another of my guns outside and do some testing, and then write up the results in my Red Notebook, where I have kept records of all my shots and the history of all my guns for many years.

I did a tremendous amount of gun testing and shooting at Red Cabin. I had the 458, a 220 Swift, my 338 OKH, a 30-'06, my old 22 Winchester M69A, a Savage-Anschutz 22 target rifle, two shotguns (12 & 20 doubles, both English), and eight handguns, from 22 to 45 Linebaugh. I shot the dickens out of all of them and made profuse notes. I had no inverter nor generator to give myself 110 volts of electricity, so once in a while I'd take my handwritten and typed notes to a friend's house or to Jack's Evergreen Lodge, set up my computer and printer, and generate some decent-looking copy for my articles.

My Alaskan handguns. On the left are four 45s. From top, 45 Linebaugh (later engraved), S&W M625, S&W M1917, and Colt 1911. Fifth from left is a custom Ruger 44, then the S&W M29, my K-22 trapline gun (here with target grips), and at the top a 38 snubby S&W M36.

Here are my rifles and two shotguns. From left, the Savage-Anschutz I refinished, a myrtle stock blank, the M69A 22, a Ruger 220 Swift, a plastic-stocked 30-'06, my incredible 338 OKH, the handy 458 I later engraved, the Double 470, and at the far right a Cogswell & Harrison 20-bore and my Hollis 12-bore duck gun.

About every two months or so I'd go to Anchorage and spend some time with my friend Danny Daniels and use his darkroom to process film and make prints. Then I'd send off a package to one or another of my markets. It all went via mail, no Internet, and it took a long time, sometimes two months, to get a response from Australia. One of the better stories I did was a piece for the 13th Edition of *Handloader's Digest* called "The 458 Revisited." It features all my loads and chronograph results, and remains one of the better pieces on the cartridge ever printed. More recently I did another definitive piece on the cartridge, featuring my engraved rifle, for the introductory pages of the 14th Edition of *Cartridges of the World*, page 44.

Here's a note I made after one such trip to town:

I absolutely love this life in the woods. I was back here from Anchorage just one day and saw a moose walk past my door. Trumpeter swans fly by. Numerous unnamed songbirds eat outside my window. A brief snowstorm; wild winds; and absolute peace and quiet. Where else in the world could I possibly live? I am immeasurably happy here and at peace.

My fox friend would generally arrive after I had made a bunch of noise with my gun testing. By the sound, he knew I was home. One day I shot my K22 revolver in the yard while he was there dozing. He kept on dozing, and that was a surprise to me. When Cookie was in the yard the birds would sit in the tree patiently. Once I had two squirrels, a handful of birds, and my fox friend in the front yard with me all at the same time. Half an hour later two caribou walked by my front door, so it was quite the menagerie. Cookie never tried to eat the other critters, nor did they attempt to interfere with him. Several times the birds would peck at things on the ground within a few feet of the fox, though the squirrels wisely stayed in the trees. They left each other completely alone, at least within my yard, so far as I knew. On my walks I'd occasionally come across a pile of grouse feathers, so I suspect Br'er Fox did in fact have a taste for something other than cat food.

Late evening as the sun goes down, two birds fly through the forest and light together on a tree, just above a man sitting on the ground under a big tree next to a small, mostly black, animal with an extremely large tail. It has a bright white tip, and the animal's nose is resting on his tail.

One bird to the other:

"Gertelbeak?"

"Yes, Bill?"

"Isn't that a man sitting there with a fox?"

"Yes, Bill."

"And isn't that fox sound asleep?"

"It sure looks like it, Bill"

"Well, I never!"

"Me neither."

And they both flew off into the forest, muttering to each other. Flap, flap, flap.

The fox opened an eye and looked at the man.

The man smiled.

The fox dozed again.

And the sun slowly sank in the northwest sky, casting a magic light on the evergreens of the north woods.

I spent some time at Evergreen Lodge helping Jack Hansen in exchange for the use of his electricity on my computer and printer. I also did some computer setup and debugging for him. One day he gave me his old John Deere JDX-8 snowmachine, which I had long coveted. I did some restoration on it, geared it down, added hand warmers, and made a thoroughly useful machine out of it. So then I had two snowmobiles, which was a blessing. Geared down, that hot-dog JDX-8 would pull the teeth out of an elephant. A snowmachine set up like that is far more useful for the bush dweller than a speedy ride that can't pull well.

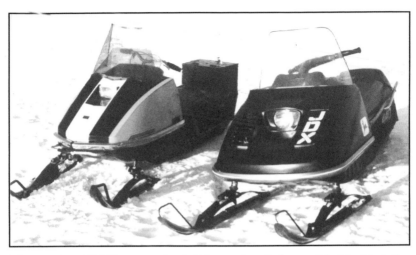

The ancient Ski-Doo on the left has a handy box added behind the seat. Jack Hansen gave me the JDX-8, which I called Black Jack. I put many hundreds of miles on these two vehicles.

Inside the cabin the dingy walls always gave me trouble seeing as well as I liked, whether for writing, gun work, checkering, or other tasks. The sun was not always cooperative, and the propane lights were not ideal for close work of any sort. Don brought me some white paint and I put it onto the inner walls, which greatly helped the lighting situation inside the cabin. With my light meter I measured the improvement to be two full stops, which means there was a whole lot more light in there than before. Another of my long-term problems was constantly running out of, or losing, pens. At the time I used ballpoints. Today I use fountain pens exclusively. To solve the problem, on one trip to Anchorage I bought seventy-two ball-point pens. They lasted a while, and I think I still had a few when I left there. Where they go has always been a huge mystery. I always seemed to have plenty of paper on hand.

In my spare time I'd read, or scratch some notes in my journal. On good days, occasional flights of fancy would come to me. Or maybe it was indigestion. I planned a magazine featuring wild animals' burrows, caves, and other dwellings. It would also discuss the things they eat. It would be called *Critter Homes and Gardens.*

Another coffee-table book would have superb photographs of the back ends of various wild animals and birds. The title would be *Tails of the North Woods.*

One day I rewrote the lyrics for "Gypsy Rover." My version:

> *He is a gypsy, my father, she cried,*
> *A crook, a pimp, and a boozer,*
> *But I will stay till my dying day,*
> *With my chiseling gypsy loser.*

First Autumn

Leaves and bushes are turning color, especially some of the fireweed. The wild rose is yellowing on the leaves and some of the "hips" are soft and edible. The blueberries are all good now, though most of those near the house have been eaten by the birds. Fall is definitely in the air, and actually is already here in the early morn and late eve.

Being commonly broke I took to being a hunter/gatherer. I did a lot more gathering than hunting. Blueberries were abundant, though not right around the cabin. My wild birds made good use of them. Elsewhere the blueberries were thick, there being not much in the way of small game around to eat them. The only rabbit I saw at Red Cabin was a baby in the talons of an eagle.

Toward the end of that first summer at Red Cabin, as my first full winter there approached, I found myself once again trying to plan a means of getting to Africa. I had long wanted to be a professional hunter there. While nothing ever came of it, I suspect I was not looking forward to another frigid winter, never mind the relative comfort I had at the cabin. I also did considerable soul-searching. I figured I belonged there in bush Alaska, so what did I need that I didn't have? This, like planning a move to Africa, was idle speculation, my mind playing tricks on me, giving me things to think about that really didn't need analyzing. I had everything I ever needed, except maybe better food and more money with which to buy it.

Then I began to look forward to hunting season. In preparation I walked here and there—finding Cookie's tracks everywhere, naming ridges and little lakes after him—and scouted for caribou, moose, and bear. I got close to a bear one day, heard him just out of sight of me, and later found his tracks, but I never saw a bear all my time there. However, the MacArthurs had a grizzly in their yard one day. Bear hunting was far more entertaining and attention-getting than chasing after caribou. It was much closer quarters, and took place in cover where I couldn't see twenty yards.

STRANGENESS

There were some mighty strange things that happened in the woods there at Red Cabin. It was passing strange, after all, that a wild old fox took a liking to me and shared so much of his life with me over all the many months I was at Red Cabin. A little later I'll tell you about the night Cookie led me into the muskeg bog on a cold night so we could be comfortable and warm together. But there were some odd things going on that are beyond me to explain. John "Pondoro" Taylor wrote of some of these sorts of things too, like the time his double hammer rifle got one of its external hammers moved to full cock while it was on his shoulder. He could never explain it.

Odd stuff seemed to happen now and then in bush Alaska. Andy Runyan, not one to tell tall tales, somewhat reluctantly told of a skull he had found along the beach near Kiavak Bay on Kodiak Island. He brought it from its resting place on the beach to his hunting cabin and parked it on a shelf there. One day shortly thereafter, the skull flew across the room. There were witnesses. Andy promptly returned the skull to its former resting place.

On one of my walks in the woods I heard an odd, fairly loud sound like a helicopter rotor near me, just behind a tree. I rushed to see what it was, rounded the tree, and saw...absolutely nothing. I had dreams that meant little to me at the time, but came to pass years later. I dreamed of wanting to play music with three guys, two guitars and a banjo, in a new neighborhood to which I had just moved. I didn't know the setting or the people, but twenty years later that dream came clearly and exactly to pass. I dreamed of the death of my mother, which also came to pass two years after I had the dream. Often I'd get a strong mental picture of one or another of my friends, or wake up thinking about them. Sometimes these were friends I had not heard from in years. Within a few days I'd have a letter from them. There were other strange things too. But perhaps strangest of all was the day I shot a caribou with my double 470.

I had been looking for a suitable caribou for some winter meat. By suitable I mean not too old, and in the right location where I could get to him easily, but not too close to the house so the offal would not draw unwelcome visitors like the bear that was wandering around. I mentioned my birds would alert me to the presence of other critters, and this day they told me—somehow—that a caribou was there, which I could not see, and that it was meant for me. Here are my notes of the event:

> I was on my way down the road to the east [hunting caribou], and had gone fifty feet or so from the cabin when something inside my mind, or maybe the birds' yelling, made me stop and ask myself, "Why not just shoot that one across the r
> I emphasize that at that time I had seen nothing, no ca
> anywhere. I turned around, walked back to the house
> then over to an open area between the house and the
> house. I started down toward the river to see if there w.
> fact, a caribou in plain sight. I still had seen nothing. Sudd
> I saw or imagined myself, or may have said to myself, '
> going to sit down, get a solid sitting shot." I then clearly in
> ined, or saw, or felt myself taking off the safety of the big
> **But I hadn't yet done that, and still had seen nothi**

Suddenly, across the river, I saw a caribou come out of the woods. It had been fully concealed until that moment. I took a step forward, sat down, got myself a solid sitting shot, took off the safety, and ... the caribou was mine.

If this was not precognition I should very much like to know what it was. I took a caribou I had not known was in the area until something told me so, and guided me into the best spot to take it. It was like I was following a pre-written or preordained script. I suspect I was not in control, just along for the ride, and I surely gave profound thanks to the powers that be. The shot, by the way, was 245 yards, not bad for a double 470 elephant rifle with iron sights, and my just-developed handload with a new powder, using my favorite paper-patched bullets. The meat provided long-term and much-needed sustenance for me that winter.

My birds told me about this caribou, which I desperately needed but didn't know was in the area. The rifle is my double 470 Churchill. The shot was taken at 245 yards.

AGAINST ALL REASON

Many have said that only humans can reason. I'll challenge that. One or two of my wild bird friends repeatedly proved me right and proved the majority of people wrong. I'd put out some sort of treat, like chunks of bread, for instance, though that's just an example. Whatever I put out was good for the birds, though I don't recall its content exactly. There were often three chunks of food in different sizes on the porch rail there for the bird. The bird would land and immediately grab the biggest piece. Then instead of immediately flying off and leaving the rest for someone else, he'd stop, look carefully at the three pieces and think about it for a second. Then he'd put the big one down and, in order of size, pick the smallest, then the middle one, and finally the biggest, according to the shape of his open beak. Then, with all three pieces on board, he'd fly off with his plunder. Several of my birds did that, time and again, and if it's not reasoning I'd again very much like to know what you'd call it.

The family of jays that lived across the river to the south were usually driven off by the family that lived near the cabin. When the near-cabin birds were temporarily absent, the outlying birds would swoop in, grab some food, and stash it in a tree fifty yards away, in line with their home across the river. Then they'd come back for more and do the same thing. When the cabin birds again chased them away, the cross-river birds would calmly carry their stashed food across the river to their home, a few hundred yards away. Pretty good reasoning for a "stupid" bird, I'd say.

More Cookie

THE ODD NOISE

I had heard a strange sound many nights. I heard it first during the late winter and early spring when I first moved into Red Cabin. I heard it up and down the river, never too near the cabin. I thought it was some sort of owl, but could never place the sound exactly, and I can't begin to describe it accurately. When I first heard it, it gave me chills. It had an unearthly quality. It was the sort of sound one might expect from a small werewolf. I'd never seen small—nor big—werewolves there at that time. It was a sort of raspy, drawn-out *Raiaannngggg!* sort of sound. One evening that late fall I heard it whilst typing a letter, and decided it was time to sneak up on its source and, once and for all, discover what was making that odd call. It seemed to be coming from the river crossing. I grabbed my shotgun (I never, ever, ventured away from home unarmed) and snuck cautiously down the road, swiftly at first, and then step by quiet step, toward the sound, which rang out again and again from that area. Two hundred yards from it, the sound was pretty loud. Must be a *huge* bird! Then I was within a hundred yards of the source. If the bird flew I hoped to get a glimpse of it. Never before had I been I so close. Only a few steps now. The bushes near the crossing hid me from the source, and the damp ground muffled my approach. Suddenly, the call again ripped through the air. ***RRIIAANNGGGHGGGGGG!*** The volume of sound nearly blew my hat off. I crept slowly around the last few bushes, and noted what seemed to be a small animal on the ground next to a tree, near where the road dropped into the river.

Could it be . . . ?

Was it . . . ?

Yes.

It was Cookie.

I had heard an odd noise. Then I saw a small dark animal under a tree. . . .

He was about as embarrassed as I was surprised. After he made sure it was me he explained that he had in fact been the source of those odd sounds all along, but never did he tell me why he was making them. I suspected it might have been that time of year when foxes go about creating new foxes, but I never knew for sure. At any rate, he gave up singing for the night and came home with me. We walked the quarter-mile back to the cabin together, he hunting the bushes along the road, I still stunned that a tiny fox could fill the world with such a tremendous volume of sound. So there we were, a man with a shotgun, and his fox friend acting much like a puppy, hunting together. I told him I thought God was smiling on us. He agreed.

From my journal notes: Fox Tactics—

If I learn nothing else from my fox friend I should learn how to deport myself in a hostile world. He trusts nothing and no one. He walks the edges of the road. He crosses the road when it is obvious (to me) he should go down it. He sits behind a tree and by not moving is invisible. (When he does this and then chooses to reveal himself I invariably feel embarrassed that I did not see him right there in plain sight.) He won't move into or through an open area without "freezing" and inspecting it. If something twitches or catches his eye, like a bird, he won't move until he has identified the object. I have seen him frozen for upward of a minute when a bird's wing had fluttered. Only when the bird again moved did he move, now knowing positively what was there.

Cookie trusted no one and nothing. He followed excellent tactics, which is why he was an old fox. He looked magnificent in winter.

As he eats he periodically stops and listens. He often moves away from his dish out to the road to listen better. If I talk too much he moves away from me, the better to hear approaching danger. He seems to direct his attention down toward the crossing, which is the opposite way from his retreat direction. When he rounds a tree or a blind corner he keeps his distance, knowing that something might be lurking 'round the corner that could grab him. (These are exactly the principles taught by my old friend Jeff Cooper at the Gunsite training center.)

Contrast his behavior with mine. I waltz around, never looking to see what might be there (unless I'm hunting, or walking in the woods). I could easily walk up to a hidden moose or bear (or elephant or lion, etc.) unaware of the danger. I tend to watch the tracks rather than look for the game that made 'em. (This is a holdover from my trapping days, when it was imperative to watch the tracks. No tracks, no traps.) Often I blunder outside blindly. Yet I've seen moose within a "kick" of the house, have scared caribou out of the yard, and one time nearly stepped on a porcupine just outside the front door.

Something deadly can come at us at any time. My fox friend knows this and lives it. That is why he is an old fox. We would all do well to emulate him and remember the above statement. There is much that is deadly in today's world, not only in bush Alaska.

One night it became perfectly clear to me that Cookie could perfectly understand my thoughts and softly spoken words, and of course had done so since the first day he saw me. Here's how it happened.

I had taken to sitting outside with Cookie after we had both eaten, and we'd doze together in the evening, sometimes for half an hour or more. We had been accustomed to sitting in the front yard, near the road. One night we were disturbed by the late passage of MacArthur's car on his way home. Cookie went north into the woods and I went south into the cabin, our communing rudely ended. The next night at dusk as we sat together, he got up and came over to get my attention and then walked down a few steps toward the river and sat down, much closer to the river than where we usually sat. I said out loud to him, "Why don't we go down toward the river?" He immediately got up, and I got the impression that that is what he had wanted to do also. I said softly, "I can't see where I'm going." It was getting dark, and walking there was not easy, even in broad daylight. He turned toward the river and walked a few paces and sat down. I walked up to him directly, and found it to be easy walking. He then went a few yards in another direction and again sat and waited until I got near him, then he'd move again.

As I followed him it was all very easy walking. He was showing me the way, leading me, fully aware that I could not see as well as he could. Finally he got to an open area and pranced back and forth, demonstrating how nice it was in that area, and then lay down. Indeed it was nice there. At my feet was a raised knoll of dry grass, to which he had guided me. I sat down a few feet from where he lay and found it to be warm and dry. Later, after he left, I took a couple steps in several directions and immediately went into a wet, boggy spot. Without his guidance I could not have got there.

In the spot to which he had led me a passing car would not disturb us, and it was wide-open ground so he could see in all directions. As we sat there the sky darkened and the stars came out. We sat together a long time in silence and enjoyed the peaceful night and the incredibly beautiful sky together. We heard fish jumping in the river. A loon called a mile away. Pretty soon I could no longer see him, just a darker area in the darkness. Some time later he got up, stretched, looked around, and then I watched his luminescent white tail tip bouncing and weaving across the muskeg as he followed the sun along the river to the west.

Cookie would eat out of my hand. One night he led me into a bog full of peace and quiet.

I sat there a long time after I could no longer see him, wondering about it all, savoring what had just happened. My friend had understood my thoughts and had led me, through what by daylight was a muskeg bog extremely difficult to navigate, to a dry spot he knew was there. Once again I was in awe of the gift I had just received.

Another evening my fox friend and I were sitting in the yard, dozing, and I thought I'd try something new. My notes:

> Two nights ago we were sitting there [in the front yard] and there was not a breath of wind. I decided to play "mouse" with him. I got his attention by peering around my tree on both sides, pretending to hide, much as I had done with my cat. Then I rustled my fingers in the grass making "mouse" sounds. He came to about four feet away and sat down, intent on the sounds. I'd rustle and he'd nearly

pounce. We did this for some minutes, the closest we've come to playing.

Often in my long walks looking for game on the surrounding ridges and valleys I'd look for his tracks to see if he had maybe been there. Often he had. Across the river to the south a long ridge ran parallel to the river. I walked it many times, and always saw the tracks of my friend there. That area became Cookie's Ridge, and a small lake behind it is Cookie's Lake, which is not far from Ray's Lake, which I had named a decade before while trapping, much as many of our western place names were bestowed by early trappers. One night at dusk I was walking home from a scouting trip, coming down the road toward the cabin from the west, head hung low, dejected about everything. I looked up, and here came Cookie up the road to meet me, happy as a lark, bouncing, and as friendly as could be. I had just dewormed him, and he was feeling pretty good. He raised my spirits immensely. In fact he did that every time I saw him. I can't thank him enough for having pulled me out of the dregs of depression so many times.

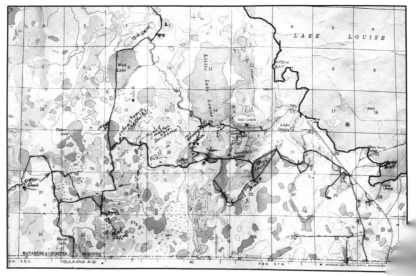

Part of my old trapline and some hiking trails from Red Cabin. trapline ran about 100 miles.

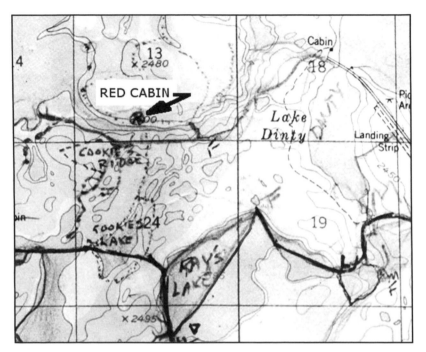

A closer view of the location of Red Cabin shows Cookie's Ridge and Ray's and Cookie's Lakes to the south of it.

Yes, I dewormed him. I took a stool sample to a vet in town and had it analyzed, and when the girl there asked me what type of dog I had, I mumbled something. But she really needed to know, and also how much he weighed, so I explained to her the medicine was not exactly for a dog. She could hardly stop giggling as she gave me what I needed. It turned out to be the correct dosage, and my little friend quickly became as happy as I'd ever seen him. He never did his business near the house. I had to search long and hard for the sample to take to town. But after he got rid of his worms he left me some good evidence in the road right in front of the cabin to show me the bugs were all gone.

After dinner we'd sit in the yard and listen to the sounds of the wilderness. He was happier after I dewormed him.

ACTIVITIES

Jack Hansen had become smarter than many another Alaskan bush dweller in his maturity, and went south, out of Alaska, for the worst months of winter. There was no reason to keep his lodge open for one or two visitors, and fight freezing water pipes in the cold. Before Jack headed south that winter I spent some time with him in his shop. He was making things on his wood lathe. I was grinding the bottom rails off my Springfield 458 to make it feed. I spent one entire day there on my 458, trying this and that, and when I was done the rifle fed perfectly, slow or fast, in any position.

Jack had given me a snowmobile, and I wanted to do something for him. He had a 22 rifle, a Stevens Model 56, which I took home, refinished, and checkered while he was gone. It turned out pretty well. On Jack's return to the lake he picked up his now checkered 22 rifle and was amazed at how good it looked. Heck, I had been checkering for over twenty years at the time, so it was no surprise to me, and it was good to give him something back

Another day I went to his shop and used his metal lathe to make two spare firing pins for my 470, some spares for his 22 Stevens, and one for another of my rifles. I knew how to heat-treat them, and they all worked just fine. On another trip there I made myself a small engraving hammer. It has served me well many years now. I copied the hammer of the master engraver Lynton McKenzie, a photo of which was on the cover of the August 1977 *The American Rifleman*, in which my gun writing had first appeared. Zen? Karma? Dunno.

I had been testing the new Barnes X-Bullets for Randy Brooks, who ran Barnes Bullets, Inc. He sent me samples of brand-new bullet concepts for my 458 and 338 OKH, and I shot them into snow, water, bone and other media, and sent him my evaluations. Generally these bullets worked extremely well, judging from the recovered samples I pulled out of my snowy bullet trap. Penetration was excellent, the bullets opened easily but in a controlled manner, and retained their weight well. One suggestion Randy acted on was putting a crimping groove onto the bullets, which they didn't have back then. The terrific recoil of the 458 mandated it.

During the winter there were huge piles of snow that Don MacArthur shoved off the road. I stacked snow into a series of mounds or baffles with holes between the mounds. I could then shoot into them and see how far the bullets had traveled by tracking the holes from mound to mound. That's how I recovered the X Bullets. I shot many cast pistol bullets into that trap and would recover them from the snow in good enough condition that I could shoot them again. Enough grease was still on them, and they had only the rifling marks for blemishes. They shot quite well the second time through the gun. Some got used three times.

I bought a chronograph for my work. It was an Oehler 35P, with so-called proof screens, and it did great service for me at Red Cabin. Finally I knew what my 458, 470, and all my handgun loads were doing. It allowed me to fine-tune my 470 loads, which for a rifle of that type was a great help. For many years I had been entirely in the dark about bullet speeds, but not anymore.

That chronograph still serves me for my regular gun testing nearly twenty-five years later. That's what I call good stuff, a fine product.

When winter arrived in earnest we soon had a spell of severe cold that left me horridly depressed. One's ambition goes entirely away at such times. My poor chickadees could hardly croak at me in the mornings. Somehow they all survived, as far as I could tell, and I hope I did them some good. Cold spells like that always made me think I was wasting time, wasting my life in an environment in which I could accomplish nothing. Such weather is always frustrating. However, I eventually realized I had accomplished a good deal during my time there. I learned things at Red Cabin that have held me in good stead all my life. That knowledge helped me get the best-paying job I've ever had, senior staff editor for DBI Books and editor of their annual, *Handguns*. It also led to my present job as senior technical editor for *Gun Tests* magazine, which I've held for seventeen years. At Red Cabin I even learned a new skill.

Engraving

When it got briefly warm that winter I found some ambition and got busy with a new project, which was learning how to engrave. I had bought James Meek's *The Art of Engraving* from Brownells nearly twenty years before. I had had an interest in engraving, tried it, and fumbled. This time I was serious, and managed to learn it quite well. I finally bought some gravers. Some months previously I had engraved my personal monogram into the gold escutcheon on my double 470. I had used what amounted to a bludgeon to do the work, yet the work had come out well. That was highly encouraging, so with both time and determination available I dug in. I spent a few weeks drawing scrolls, and less than a week after I got a decent graver and was cutting steel on some old rifle parts. It looked pretty good, so I knew I was on the right track. From the start I preferred small English scrolls, which was natural because of my affinity for early British rifles. After a brief time engraving I found myself doing things unconsciously with the graver, turning it this way and that, making little movements with it that I had no training in. I didn't know why I was doing what I was doing, but it seemed natural. They were the right movements and my engraving looked better and was more easily accomplished as a result. I wondered where I got the knowledge. Had I been an engraver in an earlier life?

One of my notes at the time: "It would be nice to be able to engrave a favorite rifle with my critters, Woody, the other birds, and of course a certain fox . . . not forgetting mice, and larger rodents (squirrels). A gun full of critters. The 458 would be an appropriate canvas."

Less than a month after I got my first good graver I began work engraving my 458. By that time it was fast becoming my number-one favorite rifle. It was light enough to carry, had great power, and I knew its ballistics were good from the use of my new chronograph. I had worked it over so it fed and functioned perfectly, and I really liked that rifle. I cut in the caliber marking, a plate for my monogram, and then started on a portrait of Buzzard the gray jay sitting in my hand. I put my old Tiger cat with her missing ears on it, and my squirrel friend Rhodent. Eventually the rifle also got portraits in cut steel of Woody, Peepkin, Snowflake the black-capped chickadee, a little mouse, and a pine grosbeak, all surrounded with scrollwork, and with banners holding most of their names.

There was a small hole in the floorplate, which I used as the mouse's little cave. The last image I put onto the big rifle, right in the middle of the floorplate, was a portrait done in "bulino" style of my fox friend Cookie. All told, it took me three months to engrave the rifle. I signed it under the barrel with my name and "Spring 1992, Alaska." I had put an image of a Cape buffalo on it, and engraved the trigger guard with "Friends + 1." Several years later in Michigan I rust blued the rifle.

With the rifle done to my satisfaction, short of its final bluing, I decided to engrave a handgun. The clear choice was the power-house I had carried on most of my excursions in the hills around Red Cabin. That was my Linebaugh 45, John's serial number 21. I had to first flatten it with stones and then proceeded to cut it. It was a lot harder or tougher steel than I had found on the 458, but I eventually got it done. It didn't get my critters, only a tombstone, because it is one of the rare "Tombstone" Sevilles. And it got a third eye and some teeth on the hammer. So in all I engraved two fire-arms at Red Cabin, both of which are still with me.

The engraving work helped greatly in passing the winter, but it was, as they always will be in Alaska, too doggoned long. It seemed winter would not go away. Another note: "Winter, dreary crone, wilt thou never leave my hearth?"

I longed to get out and be able to walk around in the hills, an activity I loved. It was the one thing I fully understood, completely related to, and truly enjoyed. My walks also included interacting with many of my bird friends, an additional joy. But please note, strenuous activity has to be approached with caution in the spring. One of the old-timers at the lake, Bob Plouffe, had a heart attack that spring, which led me to note the probable reason. Most people in Alaska vegetate all winter to some extent or another. Sleeping, reading, boozing, poor diet, you name it, are common throughout the lengthy winters there. Come good weather in the spring, everybody tries to make up for lost time by doing some strenuous activity, with a resultant overload on the ticker. For my own part I had slogged through many a snowdrift up to my waist during the winter, and had also done some cross-country skiing, so I was in better shape than most. But most Alaskan old-timers were, and are, at great risk of killing themselves in the springtime. I noted that was another reason to eventually get myself out of Alaska. I was not getting any younger, and well knew I would not be able to be nearly so active as I had been in the past, as I got older.

Winter finally and reluctantly turned to spring, and with it came the ducks, swans, and many predatory birds. I had trouble keeping all the predatory birds away from my gentle chickadees, squirrels, and gray jays. Some of my friends got eaten. Newly-arrived songbirds died from sudden cold snaps. In the peaceful surroundings I shared with my pet birds and animals the outside predators didn't belong. The only predator I allowed was Cookie, and he behaved himself. I found these deaths difficult to deal with. It made my own passage through time seem meaningless and trivial. One wants to ask, "Isn't there more? Is there some good reason for all of us living and dying? What should I be doing that I'm not? Where to? What next?"

Part of the joy of living there in the bush was seeing the new children of the various critters I knew as friends. Baby squirrels quickly made their way into my heart and my larder, as did the fresh new gray jays. The ducks had trains of young following them up and down the river. I never saw a young fox, but there must have been some. My Cookie was a male, not likely to hang out with the kids, but I seldom saw him that spring and summer, so maybe he was off taking care of a youngster or two.

"Where's dinner?" Rhodent kept me amused. I kept him fed.

In the fullness of spring I took to helping the locals work on their cabins. Don MacArthur needed help on several projects, and as I owed him money I was glad to put up with the bugs and give him some help. By some fluke I managed to get a ten-day job tagging fish on Lake Louise, which gave me a few extra dollars. And I needed all I could get, because I had decided it was time to leave.

Leaving Alaska

Late that second spring, near the end of May, I decided to leave Alaska the following fall. That left me one summer in Alaska. As noted, I worked here and there. I also patched up my Toyota, put new tires on it, and got my little travel trailer all ready to go. It took me most of the summer to arrange leaving. There was much to do, plans to be made, people to see, and the like. One nasty job was that I had to wrest one of my rifles out of the hands of a worthless so-called gunsmith who had sat on it nearly two years and had done nothing but lie to me about it. I finally got the rifle out of his shop with the help of Sherm Reynolds, though the lying gunsmith tried to prevent it. It was a 416 Rigby that I eventually completed, made feed perfectly, engraved, rust blued, and wrote up for the 1997 *Gun Digest*, the 51st Edition. I sent all my books to my mother in Michigan, some fifteen boxes of them. I sent two boxes of sixguns to John Linebaugh in Wyoming, and carried my rifles out with me.

The hardest bit of preparation was getting used to the idea of leaving all my wild friends. Today, over two decades later, rereading almost four hundred pages of my Red Cabin Journal (kept in a huge three-ring binder) was absolutely no fun. In fact it was agony. All the joy of our time together is written in my journal, and it was tough to read it all. I still miss them all, each and every one, and the agony of not ever seeing them again will be with me forever.

Whenever my thoughts return to Alaska I thank God for my time with my many friends at Red Cabin. I'm happy I could, for a time at least, provide them all with some surcease of hunger and of the pain of that killing cold, and hopefully make all their lives a little bit more enjoyable, and somewhat easier.

Hardest of all was leaving Cookie, and the peaceful times we shared.

Something inside of me seeks and needs the peace of sitting quietly under a tree, with my fox under the next one, just us guys listening to the age-old sounds of the woods. A squirrel perks Cookie's ears up. A breath of wind in the treetops makes both of us look skyward to see if, maybe, there goes a duck. A noise a mile or more away comes to our ears as we sit silently side by side . . . is it a moose? A caribou? Something more deadly—wolf? Man?

He had the most magnificent coat I've ever seen on a fox. All the good food I had provided him during the previous spring, summer, fall, and throughout winter showed in his gorgeous coat. That first summer he looked like the scrawniest little fellow imaginable, but in winter he looked better than royalty.

In the summer my friend was somewhat bedraggled and kinda scrawny looking. The bugs bothered him terribly, too.

In the slanting morning light the black fur of his back, legs, and belly is counterpointed by a golden-red glow from occasional patches of the color that most of his more common brothers wear. There are natural combed-looking ridges running along his body past his ribs. His fur is thick and rich. This is one magnificently beautiful fox.

During the summers Cookie was at least as bothered by the bugs as I was. That last summer there I tried to get some bug dope onto him, to no avail. And of course he was also not getting younger.

One warm night I looked out the window to see if he was there, and he was acting most strangely. I went out and saw him across the road, just staring at me. Then I turned around and there he was again, close to the cabin. I did a double-take, and realized there were two foxes in my yard. Cookie had brought a date! Of course I fed them both, and to this day I hope that he and his girl-friend brought some new foxes into the world with the spirit of my old rascal in their eyes.

One night I looked out and there were two foxes in the yard. Cookie brought a date!

However, I had to leave him, and I think he knew I was going. He was extremely good at reading my mind. Always had been. I think he avoided me as I made plans to go south, though maybe he was helping tend a batch of youngsters. I surely hope so. I had one good last look at him in my yard. I had fed him something, and he was happy, despite the bugs annoying him. He looked mighty good, and was healthy, far more so than when we first met. That evening he said good-bye to me with a toss of his head. He headed down the road to the west, head held high, stepping briskly, his magnificent tail flowing in the breeze. I never saw him again.

May God be with him, the little guy. My love and best wishes are with him now and forever, wherever he may roam. I wish him all the peace and happiness any fox can have on this earth, and in the next world. Cookie, my friend, my companion, my hunting partner, my teacher, my victim, my little fox.

Home at Last

I packed all my plunder into my Toyota Land Cruiser and my little travel trailer and headed south down the Alcan Highway. I went first to Wyoming, where I first set eyes on my friend John Linebaugh. I had a stack of our correspondence half an inch thick, but our first meeting was in Wyoming. I picked up my handguns from him and showed him the one he had made, his serial number 21 in 45 Linebaugh–Colt, now fully engraved. That very powerful sixgun had been a constant companion on my many hikes around Red Cabin. John liked what I had done, and said so. Then I headed to Colorado, where I spent a few days with Ross Seyfried at his ranch. Ross, who has examined more engraved firearms than most people ever see, took a long hard look at my 458. He looked at my portrait of Cookie and said, "That fox is damned good!" It was, after all, a labor of love.

The floorplate of my 458 has this image of my friend carved in steel, a labor of love.

Then it was across the country to my mother's home in Lambertville, Michigan. I was with her for nearly two years, during which I worked at two golf courses, did some gun testing, and met and acquired my one and only dog, Birdie. When Mom died of a stroke in 1994 I managed to get a job as Senior Staff Editor with DBI Books in Northbrook, Illinois. I was with them from 1994 to

1998. In 1995 I achieved my lifelong dream of getting to Africa for a Cape buffalo hunt. I took my double 470 and the 338 OKH. It was the last hunting I'll ever do.

Back at work in Illinois, every noon I'd take lunch on top of a hill in a park. From that vantage I'd look to the west with an ever-increasing longing in my heart. Despite my excellent wages, I hated being in the city with all the noise and bustle. When DBI Books was sold I found myself in a position to again leave the city behind and head west. After a diligent search over five states, and with the help of two longtime Idaho residents, Ted Keith (Elmer's son) and Tim Sundles (headman of Buffalo Bore), I found and bought my current home in the wild and rugged mountains of eastern Idaho, thirty miles from the nearest small town. I'm surrounded by mountains, trees, and with a substantial stream flowing through the middle of my property. There are no close neighbors. I have a rifle range, a few cats, and sufficient wild friends here to keep me happy.

I have finally come home. I will be here until I die, after which I suspect my spirit just might make a call up to the great North, back to Alaska to the hill on Army Point overlooking Lake Louise, and to the little cabin along the river where I found Cookie. Despite difficulties, I knew happiness and peace in my corners of wild Alaska that few people ever experience. But this time I'll have the ghosts of a little fox, a few birds, a squirrel or two, my dog, and at least one cat with me.

Index